Aging from Birth to Death

Interdisciplinary Perspectives

AAAS Selected Symposia Series

Published by Westview Press
5500 Central Avenue, Boulder, Colorado

for the

American Association for the Advancement of Science
1776 Massachusetts Ave., N.W., Washington, D.C.

Aging from Birth to Death

Interdisciplinary Perspectives

Edited by Matilda White Riley

AAAS Selected Symposium **30**

AAAS Selected Symposia Series

Copyright© 1979 by the American Association for the Advancement of Science

Published in 1979 in the United States of America by
   Westview Press, Inc.
   5500 Central Avenue
   Boulder, Colorado 80301
   Frederick A. Praeger, Publisher

Library of Congress Catalog Card Number: 78-20320
ISBN: 0-89158-363-7

Printed and bound in the United States of America

About the Book

Recent research has examined the aging process and has pointed to conditions under which the process is variable--not inevitably determined. This two-part collection reviews existing knowledge, the field, identifies interrelated social, biological, and psychological events affecting the aging process, and seeks convergence among disciplines.

The first part of the book is concerned both with specific events and with the variety of support systems and "social convoys" that affect physical and mental functioning, patterns of attitudes, and role sequences in the unfolding of individual lives. In part two, contributors consider the impact of social and environmental changes as they may shape the life-course patterns of entire cohorts of individuals born at the same time. Cohort comparisons are used to probe the variability in life-course processes. The book makes a significant contribution to both social and biomedical sciences.

About the Series

The *AAAS Selected Symposia Series* was begun in 1977 to
provide a means for more permanently recording and more
widely disseminating some of the valuable material which is
discussed at the AAAS Annual National Meetings. The volumes
in this *Series* are based on symposia held at the Meetings
which address topics of current and continuing significance,
both within and among the sciences, and in the areas in which
science and technology impact on public policy. The *Series*
format is designed to provide for rapid dissemination of
information, so the papers are not typeset but are reproduced
directly from the camera-copy submitted by the authors, without copy editing. The papers are organized and edited by
the symposium arrangers who then become the editors of the
various volumes. Most papers published in this *Series* are
original contributions which have not been previously published, although in some cases additional papers from other
sources have been added by an editor to provide a more comprehensive view of a particular topic. Symposia may be reports of new research or reviews of established work, particularly work of an interdisciplinary nature, since the AAAS
Annual Meetings typically embrace the full range of the
sciences and their societal implications.

WILLIAM D. CAREY
Executive Officer
American Association for
the Advancement of Science

Contents

List of Figures   xi

List of Tables   xiii

About the Editor and Authors   xv

PART I: AGING AND THE LIFE COURSE

Introduction: Life-Course Perspectives--
    Matilda White Riley   3

    A Conceptual Model   3
    Synopsis of the Book   5
    Plasticity in the Aging Process   6
    Social Support Over the Life
      Course   8
    Methodological Strands   9
    References   12

1 Life-Span Developmental Psychology, Cog-
    nitive Functioning and Social Policy--
    Paul B. Baltes and Sherry L. Willis   15

    Introduction   15
    Perspectives of Life-Span
      Developmental Psychology   16
      Age-Developmental Specialties Ver-
      sus Life-Span Development, 17; Onto-
      genetic Development: Personological
      Versus Contextual Conceptions, 18;
      Search for New Conceptions of
      Development, 21
    Psychometric Intelligence and
      Life-Span Development   26
      Multidimensionality, Multidirection-

*ality, and Variability,26; Multiple
Sources of Influences,29*

Life-Span Development and Social
Policy   34
*Life-Span Social Policy,34; Life-
Span Education,35*

References   38

2 The Reciprocal Effects of the Substantive
Complexity of Work and Intellectual
Flexibility: A Longitudinal Assessment
--*Melvin L. Kohn and Carmi Schooler*   47

The Longitudinal Data   49
Unreliability and Change   51
A Measurement Model for Substan-
tive Complexity   52
A Measurement Model for Intel-
lectual Flexibility   55
Causal Analysis: The Reciprocal
Effects of Substantive
Complexity and Intellectual
Flexibility   59
Discussion   69
References   73

3 Aging and Social Support-- *Robert L. Kahn*   77

Role Stress and Well-Being   79
Person-Environment Fit   81
Buffering Effect of Social
Support   82
The Convoy of Social Support   84
The Definition of Social Support   85
Convoys and Role Sets   86
Formal Properties of Convoys   87
Aging and Social Support   88
References   90

4 Social Support and Health Through the Life
Course-- *Sidney Cobb*   93

The Nature of Social Support   93
Social Support and Health   95
*During Pregnancy,95; In Early
Development,96; In Life Transitions
and Crises,96; In Specific Illness-
es,98; In Compliance with Treatment,
98; In Sparing Life,99*
Interpretations and Implications   99
References   104

PART II: AGING AND SOCIAL CHANGE

5   Aging, Social Change and Social Policy
     -- Matilda White Riley   109

     Aging and Social Change   110
       Synopsis of Part Two,111; The
       Method of Cohort Analysis,112
     Life-Course Transitions   112
     The Interplay Between Aging
       and Social Change   114
     Some Policy Implications   116
       Suggested Changes,117; Policy
       Planning and Cohort Comparison,118
     References   119

6   Intrinsic and Extrinsic Sources of Change
     in Life-Course Transitions--*Anne Foner*
     and David I. Kertzer   121

     The Age Systems of Age-Set
       Societies   122
     The Rules of Transition   123
     Role Discontinuities   125
     Transition Problems: Intrinsic
       Sources of Change   126
     Extrinsic Sources of Change
       in Transitions   128
     Conclusion   131
     Appendix A   132
     References   133

7   Changes in the Transition to Adulthood--
     Halliman H. Winsborough   137

     Previous Findings   139
     Formal Aspects of an Explana-
       tion   141
     Accounting for Changes in the
       Completion-of-Education
       Distribution: A Speculation   143
     Accounting for Change in the
       Age-at-Marriage Distribution:
       A Test of the Reflection
       Hypothesis   146
     Implications of These Results   147
     References   151

8   Demographic Change and Problems of the
     Aged--*Peter Uhlenberg*   153

      Attention to Old Age   156
      Life Course Patterns of Three
        Cohorts   158
      Conclusions   163
      References   166

9   What with Inflation and Unemployment, Who
     Can Afford to Retire?-- *James N. Morgan*   167

      Background in the Social Secur-
        ity System   167
      Retirement Situations and
        Attitudes   168
      Some Suggestive Research
        Findings   169
      Socioeconomic Change and Re-
        tirement Age   172
      The Process of Retiring   172
      The Economics of Retirement   173
      Summary   177
      References   177

10   Prospects for Aging in America--*Theodore J.
      Gordon*   179

      Introduction   179
      Study Design   181
      Curve Squaring vs. Span Ex-
        tending   183
      Biomedical Technologies   184
      Scenarios   188
      Demographic Effects   189
      Socioeconomic Consequences   191
      Social Impacts   193
      Recommendations   195

List of Figures

Chapter 1

Figure 1   Selective examples of life-span
              developmental processes   20

Figure 2   Relationship among life-span develop-
              ment, cohorts, and three major influence
              systems   24

Chapter 2

Figure 1   Measurement model for substantive com-
              plexity (final)   54

Figure 2   Measurement model for intellectual
              flexibility   56

Figure 3   The reciprocal effects of substantive
              complexity and intellectual flexibility:
              full model   60

Figure 4   The reciprocal effects of substantive
              complexity and intellectual flexibility:
              significant paths only   66

Chapter 4

Figure 1   Number of deaths before, during, and
              after birth month   100

Figure 2   An hypothesis about the nature of the
              relationship of stress and strain in the
              face of varying levels of social support   101

xii   *List of Figures*

Figure 3   An hypothesis about the mechanism
              through which social support might
              operate to improve an individual
              relationship with the environment   102

Chapter 7

Figure 1   Quartiles of the age distributions at
              school completion, first job, armed
              forces service and first marriage for
              selected birth years   138

Figure 2   Percent of five-year birth cohorts in
              each of three temporal ordering cate-
              gories by military service   140

Figure 3   Actual and expected ages at first quar-
              tile of first marriage, 1947–1969   148

Figure 4   Actual and expected ages at median age
              of first marriage, 1947–1969   149

Figure 5   Actual and expected ages at third quar-
              tile of first marriage, 1947–1969   150

Chapter 10

Figure 1   Effect of curve squaring and life-
              extending technologies   182

Figure 2   Age cohort distribution   192

List of Tables

Chapter 4

Table 1   The relationship of perceived social
support to health status of women 13
months after the death of their husbands   97

Chapter 7

Table 1   Chi-square statistics for a backward
selection of loglinear models for a
table of age by nuptiality, by period,
by school completion, by military status
for males 16-35 in 1947-1971   144

Chapter 8

Table 1   A demographic perspective on the childhood characteristics of three cohorts   160

Table 2   A demographic perspective on the adulthood characteristics of three cohorts   160

Table 3   A demographic perspective on the old age
characteristics of three cohorts   162

Chapter 9

Table 1   Monthly annuity payable with or without
continued occupancy of home   175

Chapter 10

Table 1   Life-extending technologies judged more
likely than not by the year 2000   185

Table 2   Principal concepts and approaches to
            control of aging   186

Table 3   Biomedical forecasts: key findings   187

Table 4   Summary of scenario assumptions   188

Table 5   Demographic effects   190

About the Editor and Authors

Matilda White Riley, Daniel B. Fayerweather Professor of Political Economy and Sociology at Bowdoin College, has worked extensively in research methodology and the sociology of aging. She is a fellow of the Center for Advanced Studies in the Behavioral Sciences (1978-1979) and holds a number of offices including president of the Eastern Sociological Society, chairperson of the Research Committee of the Gerontological Society, of the Social and Economic Sciences Section of the American Association for the Advancement of Science, and of the Committee on Life-Course Perspectives on Middle and Old Age of the Social Science Research Council. Her many publications on cohort analysis, age stratification, and related topics include Aging and Society *(3 vols.; Russell Sage Foundation, 1968-1972) and* Sociological Research *(2 vols.; Harcourt Brace Jovanovich, 1963).*

Paul B. Baltes, professor of human development at Pennsylvania State University, is currently carrying out research on development of ability and personality structure, cultural change and adolescent and adult personality, intervention in adult development and aging, and related topics. He is a fellow of the Gerontological Society and of the Center for Advanced Study in the Behavioral Sciences, and was president of the Adult Development and Aging Division of the American Psychological Association (1977). A recipient of the Raymond B. Cattell Award for Distinguished Research from the Society for Multivariate Experimental Psychology, Baltes serves as a consulting editor on numerous journals and has published four books, most recently, Life-Span Development and Behavior: Advances in Research and Theory, Volume 1 *(Academic Press, 1978).*

Sidney Cobb, professor of community health and of psychiatry at Brown University, has conducted extensive research in the field of psychosocial epidemiology. He is past president of the American Psychosomatic Society and is the author of numerous publications on the epidemiology of psychosomatic illness and on the effects of job termination.

Anne Foner, associate professor of sociology at Rutgers University, specializes in the areas of sociology of age and social stratification. She was on the editorial board of the Social Gerontology Section of the Journal of Gerontology *(1977) and is the author of numerous publications, including* Aging and Society, Volumes I and III *(Russell Sage Foundation):* An Inventory of Research Findings *(Volume I, with M. W. Riley, 1968) and* A Sociology of Age Stratification *(Volume III, with M. W. Riley and M. Johnson, 1972).*

Theodore J. Gordon, president of The Futures Group in Glastonbury, Connecticut, works in the areas of policy analysis, technology assessment, new venture analysis, long-range planning, and futures research. He was principal investigator of a project on life-extending technologies which resulted in the book A Technology Assessment of Life-Extending Technologies *(The Futures Group, 1976), of which he was co-author.*

Robert L. Kahn, program director at the Institute for Social Research and professor in the Department of Psychology at the University of Michigan, has worked chiefly in the area of organizational structure and behavior, particularly in relation to mental and physical health and organizational effectiveness. He serves on the editorial board of the Journal of Applied Behavioral Science, *on the Social Science Research Council's Committee on Work and Personality in the Middle Years, and on the Task Panel on Community Support Systems of the President's Commission on Mental Health (1977), and is active in the American Psychological Association. He is the author of over 100 books, monographs, and papers, including* The Social Psychology of Organizations, 2nd Edition *(with D. Katz; Wiley, 1978).*

David I. Kertzer, assistant professor of anthropology at Bowdoin College, has studied the fields of social organization, demographic anthropology, and the interrelationship of politics and religion. He was a Woodrow Wilson Dissertation Fellow and in 1978 was a Fulbright Senior Lecturer in Italy. He has published and presented a number of papers on various topics, including African age-set societies, European peasant household structure, urbanization effects on household composition, and analytical methods.

Melvin L. Kohn, chief of the Laboratory of Socio-environmental Studies at the National Institute of Mental Health, works in the field of social structure and personality. He is president of the Sociological Research Association (1978-79) and former vice president of the Society for the Study of Social Problems, and has been an associate editor of several journals. He is the author of Class and Conformity: A Study in Values *(2nd ed.; University of Chicago Press, 1977) and articles on social stratification, occupational structure, and individual psychological functioning.*

James N. Morgan, a research scientist with the Institute for Social Research and professor of economics at the University of Michigan, works primarily in the areas of behavioral economics and survey research. He is a member of the National Academy of Sciences, a fellow of the American Statistical Association, and a recipient of the University of Michigan's Distinguished Faculty Achievement Award. His numerous publications include Early Retirement: The Decision and the Experience *(with Richard E. Barfield; Univ. of Mich. Inst. for Social Research, 1969) and* Five Thousand American Families: Patterns of Economic Progress *(co-editor; 6 vols.; Univ. of Mich. Inst. for Social Research).*

Carmi Schooler, research psychologist with the Laboratory of Socio-environmental Studies at the National Institute of Mental Health, works in the area of social structure and personality. He received the Japanese Government Research Award for Foreign Specialists in 1971 and has published articles on the psychological consequences of occupational experience and of the structural and cultural antecedents of normal and abnormal adult psychological functioning.

Peter Uhlenberg is an associate professor in the Department of Sociology at the University of North Carolina. He specializes in demography and has published articles on the demography of the family and demographic aspects of aging populations. He is a Fulbright Lecturer at Seoul National University, Korea, for 1978-79.

Sherry L. Willis, associate professor in the Division of Individual and Family Studies at Pennsylvania State University, specializes in educational psychology and human development. She is a member of several professional societies and has published articles on cognitive development and intervention across the lifespan and lifelong learning and education.

Halliman H. Winsborough, professor of sociology at the University of Wisconsin-Madison, has worked extensively in the fields of demography and social statistics. He is a former director of the Center for Demography and Ecology at the University and is editor of the Population Studies Series by Academic Press. He has published on the topics of estimability of age, period, and cohorts effects and statistical histories of the life cycle of birth cohorts.

Part I
Aging and the Life Course

Introduction
Life-Course Perspectives

Matilda White Riley

Ten years ago I could not have elicited such a series of chapters for this symposium. Ten years ago, knowledge of the life course was constrained by inadequate theory, curtailed by inappropriate data, contained by chronology. Researchers even thought they could generalize about "the process" of aging from cross-section samples. They believed that both retrospective and prospective data could be taken at face value. Ten years ago, the chapters in such a symposium could have shown little or no real comprehension of time or chronicity.

Here I speak with authority and from personal experience. When the first of our three volumes on Aging and Society was published (Riley, Foner, Moore, Hess, and Roth, 1968), exactly ten years ago, this was precisely the situation. Of the countless research reports we examined for inclusion in that inventory of social science findings on the middle and later years, only a few reports met the minimum criteria for scientific research. Most were flawed by faulty theory or fallacious methodology. All too many attempted to extrapolate from static research to some kind of a dynamic aging process.

A Conceptual Model

In 1978, researchers typically make fewer such mistakes. Today our two-part symposium can benefit from a heuristic conceptual framework designed to alert us in advance to fallacious interpretations (cf. Riley, 1973), and to aid us in providing new insights into age-related phenomena over the proximate future. This framework has developed from two lines of research and theory in psychology and sociology that have begun to converge over the past decade and that now form a broad social science perspective for the study of aging over the life course. We have begun to forge links between life-span developmental psychology (as in the work of Baltes,

3

Schaie, Nesselroade, and others and specified in the chapter
in this volume by Baltes and Willis) and the sociological
analysis of age (as in my own work with Foner, Johnson, Hess,
Clausen, Brim, Waring, and others, and illustrated here in
the chapter by Foner and Kertzer). We have begun to delineate the connections with related disciplines: demographic,
historical, economic, political, biological, medical. And
this developing integration now provides a new and powerful
conceptual apparatus--a life-course perspective.

Let me list four <u>central premises</u> of this emerging
perspective:[1]

1. Aging is a life-long process of growing up and
growing old. It starts with birth (or with conception)
and ends with death.

Thus no single stage of a person's life (childhood,
middle age, old age) can be understood apart from
its antecedents and consequences (cf. Brim, 1966;
Clausen, 1972; Riley, 1971).

2. Aging consists of three sets of processes--biologi-
cal, psychological, and social; and these three processes are all systemically interactive with one another
over the life course.

Thus, as a person changes biologically, he or she
is also moving through a succession of social roles,
accumulating knowledge, developing attitudes and
patterns of behavior--social and psychological
processes which can in turn react upon the biological processes (cf. Cobb, 1976).

3. The life-course pattern of any particular person
(or cohort of persons all born at the same time) is
affected by social and environmental change (or history).

As a person is growing up and growing old, historical trends and events are occurring that can influence the patterns of his or her life (cf. Elder,
1974).

4. New patterns of aging can cause social change. That
is, social change not only molds the course of individual lives but, when many persons in the same cohort are
affected in similar ways, the change in their collective

---

[1]For fuller discussion, see Riley, Johnson, and Foner, 1972;
Abeles and Riley, 1976-77; references in subsequent chapters.

lives can in turn also produce social change (cf. Waring, 1975).

Thus there is an interdependence--a continuing interplay--between aging and social change.

In using this perspective here, we attempt to avoid certain terminological confusions. We shall speak of:

--"aging" as growing up and growing old (not confined to old age);

--"a cohort" as a set of people born (or entering a system) at approximately the same period (reserving the word "generation" for the kinship context);

--"life course" (rather than life cycle or life span, each of which has special disciplinary connotations).

Synopsis of the Book

Such common terminology and these four premises are used as compass points in the chapters of this symposium. Conceptual help is freely drawn upon for integrating the diverse strands of research from the several disciplines represented. Communication across disciplines is difficult at best. Yet it is the essence of our several premises that aging over the life course is the product of a series of interconnections among phenomena examined in discrete fields of study. Search for such interconnections gives direction to the symposium.

PART ONE is mainly concerned with aging processes at the micro-level. The chapters deal with the life course of the individual--his or her life-time pattern of behavior, attitudes, and cognitive functioning; the sequence of roles played at school, at work, or in the family; changing health and vigor. Here the symposium is guided by our first two premises--that aging is a life-long process, not limited to any particular life stage; and that aging consists of inter-related biological, psychological, and social processes.

Even though a macro-level focus is reserved for PART TWO, an attempt is also made throughout the volume to keep in mind the third and fourth premises--that each individual biography is affected by changes in the social environment, and that changes in the collective biographies of individuals affect the social environment. Social change shapes the life-course patterns of entire cohorts of individuals, since people born at the same time share the same slice of history.

Historical changes (in social and economic institutions, in values and the state of the arts, in patterns of fertility and mortality, in the purity of water and air, in wars and depressions) distinguish the life-course experiences of one cohort of individuals from those of adjacent cohorts. And in turn, as many individuals are influenced by social change to lead their lives in new ways, social norms and institutions undergo still further changes.

Quite literally, then, the symposium set for itself the bold task of elaborating a life-course perspective on the aging process. The central effort is to examine both continuities and disjunctures in a range of age-related behaviors, attitudes, feelings, and events from birth to death. The aim is to conclude with some clearer understandings of what this vexatious process of aging is all about.

Plasticity in the Aging Process

The book begins, as it will conclude, with mounting evidence that points unmistakably to conditions under which the process of growing up and growing old is variable, not inexorably determined. Despite much lore to the contrary, there is nothing inevitable about many "developments" or "decrements" stereotypically associated with aging over the life course--most poignantly in the later years. Many of the processes associated with age stem, not from any intrinsic process of aging, but from variable environmental causes or from potentially correctable pathologies. The mutability of the aging process is a major theme among the many in this book. And the challenge is to scrutinize existing knowledge, to seek explicit convergences among disciplines, and to identify those interrelated social, psychological, and biological processes and events which enable us to specify how, in what respects, to what extent, and under what conditions the process is flexible.

This challenge is accepted by Paul Baltes and Sherry Willis in their chapter on "Life-Span Developmental Psychology, Cognitive Functioning, and Social Policy." In the life-span developmental view, individuals continue to develop and change throughout their lives from birth to death, and aging is a life-long process which can only be properly understood as an outcome of life-long experience. Baltes and Willis contrast this life-span model with the traditional model used in child psychology which, closely related to the biologist's conception of growth, describes "developmental" behavior-change processes as "unidirectional, sequential, qualitative, irreversible, fairly normative..., and oriented toward an endstate (e.g., maturity)." The traditional model also displays a "benign neglect" of the impact of social change on ontogenetic change. Thus, for example, Gesell draws a parallel between maturational factors and a child's behavioral development, with little reference to external, environmental influences; or Piaget is more concerned with universal stage sequences than with cultural variability; or many students of old age attribute intellectual declines exclusively to biological factors rather than to the possible cumulation of negative environmental events.

Life-span psychologists have begun to regard such a unitary biologically-based model of development as unduly restrictive. While accepting it as one case among many, they stress the potential departures from it, as developmental functions can display multiple directions, diverse trajectories, much interindividual variability and intraindividual plasticity, and response to changes in the social and cultural environment. As an example, Baltes and Willis provide a life-span developmental view of psychometric intelligence. Multidimensionality and multidirectionality are illustrated by the distinction between crystallized and fluid intelligence, with crystallized intelligence tending to improve over much of the life span, whereas fluid intelligence fits an inverted U-shaped curve with maximum performance for most people around the third decade of life. Evidence for variability and plasticity is also adduced. Thus intellectual development varies according to people's educational level, or according to the cohorts to which they belong. Moreover, Baltes has shown that, for old people, intervention of various kinds (such as training, or manipulation of social support) can produce dramatic increases or decreases in intellectual performance. These authors conclude that "the evidence accumulated thus far is sufficiently strong to mandate a search for alternative conceptions of adult psychometric intelligence."

Other studies probe behind the apparent plasticity of the aging process in the search for underlying causal mechanisms. Clearly, it is not enough to observe age-related variations in psychometric intelligence and other life-course behaviors and attitudes; further research is needed to identify the antecedent factors in such life-course variations. As Baltes and Willis note, Jarvik et al. (1973) have pointed to antecedent factors in the social structure that are associated with age patterns of verbal ability (an important measure of intellectual functioning). Stability and even increase in verbal ability during most of the adult life course appear to be related more to an individual's educational background or to the intellectual stimulation available in the current environment than to age per se.

An important causal link in this relationship between
social structure and psychological functioning is demonstrated
in this volume in the chapter by Melvin Kohn and Carmi
Schooler. Addressing one aspect of the basic question
whether social structure affects personality only through its
influence on childhood socialization or also through a continuing influence during the entire life course, Kohn and
Schooler report findings from their own ten-year longitudinal
study of adult males. They examine the reciprocal relationship between one dimension of occupational structure, the
substantive complexity of work, and one dimension of psychological functioning, intellectual flexibility. Their research
method, structural equation causal analysis, is complex and
sophisticated, and their findings are impressive. They show
that the effect of substantive complexity of work on intellectual flexibility is remarkably strong--on the order of one-
fourth as great as the effect of men's earlier levels of
intellectual flexibility on their present intellectual flexibility. As one might expect, the reciprocal effect of intellectual flexibility on substantive complexity is even more
pronounced. This reciprocal effect is not contemporaneous,
but is rather a "lagged" effect that occurs gradually over
time. Thus it seems clear that people do not simply fit into
and perhaps mold their jobs as they age; their intellectual
functioning is also affected by these jobs. In a dynamic
sense, the quality of living appears to be related to the
quality of the workplace.

Social Support Over the Life Course

Patterns of stability and change with aging can also be
markedly affected by availability of social support, a topic
to which two chapters are addressed. Robert Kahn, writing on
"Aging and Social Support," speaks of each individual as
moving through life surrounded by a "social convoy," a set
of significant others who give or receive such forms of social
support as affect, affirmation, and aid. The term "social
convoy" is both colorful and arresting. It implies movement--
for example, a movement from school to work, a change of jobs,
retiring, or a change in the convoy itself as through divorce
or death of a spouse. Thus the convoy of the new-born infant
may be restricted largely to parents and siblings, characterized by asymmetry as the infant receives many kinds of
social support while giving in return little but emotional
rewards of parenthood. In young adulthood and middle age the
size and symmetry of the convoy may increase, contracting
again in very old age. Kahn summarizes relevant earlier
research in which social support serves both as a direct
reducer of stress or strain, and as a buffer or moderating
variable between stress and strain. He then notes plans for

future research focusing on the formal structure of social convoys at different points in the life course, and on the conditions under which properties of the convoy may determine mental and physical well-being, performance in major social roles, and success in managing life changes and transitions.

Sidney Cobb's chapter on "Social Support and Health through the Life Course" extends Kahn's theme of social support systems, and specifies the impact of such systems on various age-related health problems during gestation and at birth, in early development, at times of life crises, in bereavement, and at the point of one's own death. Cobb's argument is based on his review of a wide range of studies which, though they differ in objectives and research procedures, all examine the relationship between some form of social support and some criterion of ill health, such as: complications of pregnancy, low birth weight, childhood achievement of bladder control, depression, tuberculosis, arthritis, and coronary heart disease. In most instances, Cobb notes an observed association between low social support and pathological symptoms, consistent with the hypothesis that this special feature of the social environment can protect against ill health and can facilitate recovery. Part of the facilitation of recovery is mediated by the patient's improved compliance with medical prescriptions, an improvement that is in itself strongly associated with the availability of social support. More generally, Cobb argues that social support reduces the impact of stress by encouraging both adaptation (enabling the individual to alter his or her needs) and coping (changing the environment to meet these needs). It is a far-ranging argument, involving the interplay between the physiological and the psycho-social components of the aging process (our second premise for a life-course perspective); and the implications for reducing the health-related decrements at all ages over the life course are compelling.

Methodological Strands

These themes of variability in the life-long aging process, and of the social support systems that can channel the variability, only begin to illustrate the range of research objectives defined by students of the life course. Guided by the broad framework of our conceptual model, and serving to specify and elaborate this model, these diverse objectives can be seen as imposing many special requirements on research designs for assembling, analyzing, and interpreting empirical data (cf. Riley, Johnson, and Foner, 1972, Appendix).

Some of the simpler research designs treat age itself as an independent variable, describing its relationship to a particular behavior, attitude, characteristic, or other selected feature of the life course. Yet, as Baltes and Willis point out, chronological age is at best a "preliminary index of developmental change." When the aim is to understand even one selected feature of the life-course pattern, such as entering the first marriage (as in the later chapter by Winsborough), researchers are rarely satisfied by merely knowing at which age this event occurred, or whether it occurred at all. Also important is information about the life-course sequence of surrounding events--such as completing school, starting work, leaving the parental home, marrying, having a child; as well as information about the elapsed time--the time spent in each step in the sequence, and the waiting time between steps.

Certain research objectives require tracing the paths of antecedents and consequences of selected life-course events, and probing the causal linkages. On occasion, the classical experimental design is useful here. For example, Baltes and Willis describe intervention research in which older persons (aged 59-85) were first tested, then subjected to eight one-hour training sessions dealing with one component of fluid intelligence ("figural relations"), then tested again. This experiment reportedly resulted in marked improvement in the tests involved, an improvement transferred also to tests on other domains of intelligence (with the transfer-of-training effect maintained at a follow-up six months later). Just as training, incentives, or other factors can be experimentally manipulated for their effects on test performance, social support is also amenable to experimentation, as the chapters by Cobb and by Kahn imply. Kahn proposes to vary the types of social support or the size of social "convoys," for example, in field research to clarify the causal connections with various indicators of well-being.

Since experiments with human beings are often neither feasible nor ethical, however, special analytical devices are often employed for examining factors viewed as causal. Among these devices is the use of structural equation models (appropriately described as "path analysis" in the life-course connection), elegantly illustrated in the chapter by Kohn and Schooler. These researchers employ computer techniques (developed by Jöreskog), which allow study of both "contemporaneous effects" of one variable on another and "lagged effects" that occur more gradually over time. These techniques have the added advantage of combining the causal analysis with tests for measurement error ("maximum likelihood confirmatory factor analysis"). The measurement tests

are especially important in longitudinal studies such as
this one, where it must be demonstrated that an apparently
real change, as in intellectual functioning, is not entirely
an artifact of repeated measurement.

Many research objectives, and the associated procedures
for measurement and analysis, pose special difficulties in
obtaining the data. The entire lifetime of a human being, unlike that of a fruitfly or a mouse, cannot readily be encompassed by the researcher (who may himself die sooner than
the subject being observed). Hence students of aging have
recourse to a variety of data-gathering strategies, each
with its own strengths and weaknesses. One strategy is to
dovetail into a synthetic life-course view a set of short
longitudinal studies of people who start out at differing
ages at Time 1; this procedure reduces waiting time for the
researcher but overlooks the potentially confounding differences among the cohorts being pieced together. Another
strategy is secondary analysis of data already available. Reanalysis of studies already completed by other researchers
provides the basis for the chapters by Cobb and by Foner
and Kertzer, for example. By examining existing ethnographic
reports, Foner and Kertzer create a test-tube of pre-literate,
age-graded societies within which to consider aging as it
concerns us today. Several other studies in PART TWO illustrate the currently increasing use of computerized data from
past surveys or censuses. Such data rarely meet the
researcher's objectives in full (e.g., Winsborough complains
that adequate information on fertility is available only for
females, not for males). Yet available data can often afford
large samples and unparalleled command over distant times
or places.

Secondary analysis may be particularly useful when the
life course is to be examined in relation to social change,
the major theme of PART TWO. Micro-level analyses, as illustrated here in PART ONE, are often ahistorical. Wide socio-
temporal variations are not pertinent to many research objectives that deal with our first two premises: that aging is
life-long and comprises interrelated social, psychological,
and biological processes. Massive historical data are not
needed in these chapters to demonstrate that the pattern of
aging is not immutable, or that the nature of a man's work
can influence his intellectual performance, or that emotional
support and affection can make the difference between sickness
and health. Nevertheless, other important questions remain
unanswered in these studies. How variable are life-course
patterns of health and illness, of cognitive functioning, of
motivation to work, of political participation, of desiring
children, of fearing death? Under what conditions of time and

place does training in cognitive skills or provision of
social support make a difference? What societal consequences
follow upon many collective life-course decisions to marry
early and produce a "baby boom" cohort? Why do cohorts
differ from one another in performance on psychometric
tests?--a tantalizing question left open by Baltes and Willis.
How do historical changes in the medical conditions surrounding pregnancy and birth affect early and subsequent development of neonates?

Such questions press for use of the historical dimension,
for research that transcends the lifetime of a single cohort
and draws comparisons among successive cohorts. Research
on the past and the future, using cohort comparisons, will be
presented in PART TWO of this symposium.

References

Abeles, Ronald P. and Matilda White Riley, 1976-77. "A
    Life-Course Perspective on the Later Years of Life: Some
    Implications for Research." Social Science Research
    Council Annual Report. New York: Social Science Research
    Council, pp. 1-16.

Brim, Orville G., Jr., 1966. "Socialization Through the Life
    Cycle," in Orville G. Brim, Jr. and Stanton Wheeler,
    Socialization After Childhood: Two Essays. New York:
    Wiley, pp. 1-49.

Clausen, John A., 1972. "The Life Course of Individuals,"
    in Matilda White Riley, Marilyn Johnson, and Anne Foner,
    Aging and Society, III: A Sociology of Age Stratification.
    New York: Russell Sage Foundation, pp. 457-515.

Cobb, Sidney, 1976. "Social Support as a Moderator of Life
    Stress." Psychosomatic Medicine, 38 (5), pp. 300-314.

Elder, Glen H., Jr., 1974. Children of the Great Depression:
    Social Change in Life Experience. Chicago: University
    of Chicago Press.

Jarvik, L., C. Eisdorfer, and J. Blum (eds.), 1973.
    Intellectual Functioning in Adults. New York: Springer.

Riley, Matilda White, 1971. "Social Gerontology and the Age
    Stratification of Society." The Gerontologist, 11 (1),
    pp. 79-88.

Riley, Matilda White, 1973. "Aging and Cohort Succession:
    Interpretations and Misinterpretations." Public Opinion
    Quarterly, 37 (Spring), pp. 35-49.

Riley, Matilda White, Anne Foner, Mary E. Moore, Beth Hess, and Barbara K. Roth, 1968. Aging and Society, I: An Inventory of Research Findings. New York: Russell Sage Foundation.

Riley, Matilda White, Marilyn Johnson, Anne Foner, 1972. Aging and Society, III: A Sociology of Age Stratification. New York: Russell Sage Foundation.

Waring, Joan M., 1975. "Social Replenishment and Social Change," in Anne Foner (ed.), American Behavioral Scientist, 19 (2), pp. 237-256.

Any full list of references--too long
a list for this highly focused symposium--
would include distinguished scholars who
have contributed in diverse and important
ways to the development of a life-course
perspective. Some of these are included
in the references to other chapters.

Life-Span Developmental Psychology, Cognitive Functioning and Social Policy

1

Paul B. Baltes and Sherry L. Willis

Introduction

The purpose of this chapter[1] is to present a life-span developmental perspective of the aging process in psychology. Recent expressions of a life-span orientation are combined in a growing number of publications such as the West Virginia Conferences on life-span developmental psychology (Baltes & Schaie, 1973; Goulet & Baltes, 1970; Datan & Ginsberg, 1976; Datan & Reese, 1977; Nesselroade & Reese, 1973) or the appearance of a new annual series entitled Life-Span Development and Behavior (Baltes, 1978).

A life-span developmental approach maintains that individuals continue to develop and change across the life course. Aging, then, is viewed as a life-long process which can only be properly studied as an outcome of life-long experiences. A life-span view of human development and aging has also contributed to the perspective that individual development occurs in the context of biocultural change. Thus, the process of aging must involve examination of the relationship between ontogenetic-individual development and social change across the entire lifetime. The biocultural context may be seen as involving both micro-level, individual life events and macro-level, ecological and social events. This particular approach

[1]Preparation of this manuscript was supported by a grant from the National Institute on Aging (# 5 R01 A00430-02) to both authors. The first author also acknowledges with gratitude many informal contributions from colleagues participating in the work of a Social Science Research Committee on Life-Course Perspectives on Middle and Old Age, particularly from Orville G. Brim, Jr., Glen H. Elder, and Matilda White Riley. In addition, Bernice L. Neugarten made valuable comments on an earlier draft of this manuscript.

involving a linkage between ontogenetic and social change has benefited much from similar developments in the sociological literature (e.g., Elder, 1975; Riley, 1976; Riley, Johnson & Foner, 1972).

In this paper, basic tenets of a life-span developmental approach will be discussed and contrasted with the orientation of traditional developmental psychology. Although a life-span approach is being applied to an increasing variety of aspects of development and aging, we will draw our research examples from the area of intellectual functioning. Primary attention will be given to the relationship between individual development and the biocultural context at descriptive and explanatory levels. Our basic position will be that the study of aging requires a life-span perspective extending from birth to death and that discussion of the sources of developmental aging must include examination of the biocultural (ecological) context as well as intraorganismic factors.

Finally, some generic implications of a life-span perspective for the development of social policy will be reviewed. The key assumption for the possibility of an interface between social policy and life-span developmental psychology is that social policy represents application of knowledge from a variety of disciplines, and developmental psychology is one of the behavioral specialities that can contribute to this task. Social policy, then, is seen to benefit from a human development orientation and an explicit concern with efforts at intervening into and optimizing the course of ontogenetic development (e.g., Baltes & Danish, 1978, in press). Since social policy is a multifaceted area, the field of education has been chosen as a sample case for the kind of perspectives which a life-span developmental view might contribute.

Perspectives of Life-Span Developmental Psychology

In our view, a life-span developmental psychology is less a theory than a perspective or an orientation which suggests, on a fairly abstract level, a unique set of theoretical and methodological paradigms. Developmental psychology, as a field in the behavioral sciences, is defined as dealing with the descriptive and explanatory study of individual development of behavior, i.e., ontogenetic psychological development. There are two themes in the history of developmental psychology which are helpful as background for discussing the distinguishing features in the emerging life-span developmental orientation in psychology.

Age-developmental Specialities versus Life-span Development

One historical theme deals with the paradox that developmental psychology has not evolved as a full-fledged life-span or life-course conception of individual development. Rather, except for the recent decade, developmental psychology evolved largely as a set of distinct, age-bracketed specialties: infant development, child development, adolescence, adulthood, aging. All of these age specialities of developmental psychology have managed to formulate their own bodies of knowledge with little cross-fertilization and ontogenetic linkage. This is particularly true for the two specialities which are probably the most advanced: child psychology and the psychology of aging (known in their multidisciplinary conceptions as child development and gerontology). An example of this age-segmented approach is reflected in the psychometric framework of intellectual assessment. Global intelligence measures such as the Wechsler and Stanford-Binet involve age-graded tests, each grade level of the test seeking to evaluate knowledge and skills deemed specific to that particular age segment, rather than assessing the individual's changing understanding of the same concept across different developmental periods. Moreover, the concept of intelligence has been largely one of childhood and early adulthood intelligence (Schaie, 1979, in press) with little attention paid to unique features of adult-developmental processes (see Riegel, 1973, and, Schaie, 1977, for notable exceptions).

It is amazing for the historical observer that such an age-fragmentation of the field of developmental psychology could occur, because there is neither an immediate historical nor any conceptual justification. On the one hand, it has recently been shown that the early 18th and 19th century origins of developmental psychology were primarily life-span and not child developmental conceptions (Baltes, 1979, in press; Reinert, 1976). On the other hand, despite the presumed conceptual focus of developmental psychology on behavior-change processes, it seems surprising that the major lines of age-specific implementation involved fairly atemporal, static, rather than processual, conceptions of development. Somehow, science-irrelevant factors, such as child-oriented features peculiar to most Western societies, and various contextual-political conditions such as funding mechanisms, must have prevented the earlier conceptual purity of a life-span approach from coming to fruition until recently.

The last decades, however, have seen a major re-orientation in this regard, following the lead of such programs as those at the University of Chicago in the United States (e.g., Committee on Human Development, 1965) and at the Uni-

versity of Bonn in Germany (e.g., Thomae, 1979, in press).
Increasingly, it is being recognized that the study of behavioral development is either incomplete or seriously hampered
unless it is seen in the context of the life-span or life-
course (see also Lerner & Ryff, 1978). Thus, life-span developmental psychology has come to provide a conceptual umbrella
under which separate age-developmental specialties can be
located and integrated. A life-span model seeks to examine
the interrelationship among developmental periods or developmental processes and to define patterns or sequences of developmental changes. Indeed, in contrast to an age-specific
approach where the significance of chronological age is para-
mount, a life-span approach with its emphasis on developmental
patterns across the life-course does not necessarily dictate a
close association between all developmental sequences and
chronological age. In fact, for certain psychological processes such as intellectual functioning in adulthood, chronological age may be a less than useful preliminary index of
developmental change. For example, stability or even increase
in verbal ability (an important measure of intellectual functioning) during most of the adult life span appears to be more
related to the individual's educational background or to the
intellectual stimulation available in the current environment
than to age per se (Jarvik et al., 1973). Similarly, as is
persuasively shown by Schaie (1979, in press), in the current
cohorts of older people, there appears to be more variance in
intellectual performance associated with birth-cohort than
with chronological age.

Ontogenetic Development: Personological vs Contextual Conceptions

The emphasis on ontogenetic-individual development tradi-
tionally employed by developmental psychologists deals with
only one type of behavioral change, i.e., with that behavior-
change process which can be discerned when following persons
over extended periods of time. There are other types of behavior change which are often disregarded by developmental
psychology. Of particular interest to other social scientists,
but excluded from the territory of traditional developmental
psychology, are those types of behavioral change which are
related to species (evolutionary) development and to biocultural social change. This observation is most conspicuous if
one attends to concerns of sociologists interested in aspects
of human development and social change (Elder, 1975; Riley,
1976; Riley et al., 1972; Keniston, 1971).

Indeed, traditional developmental psychology's benign
neglect of these other change phenomena may have seriously
limited the psychological study of ontogenetic change. That

is, lack of concern for the biocultural context in which the
individual develops may have resulted in an over-emphasis on
age-segmented, normative, intraorganismic (personological)
models of development (see also Bronfenbrenner, 1977; Riegel,
1976). Characteristics of such normative, personological
developmental models will be briefly summarized to provide
later contrast with the life-span approach and its contextual
emphasis. Note for heuristic and didactic reasons, the
following presentation is purposefully accentuated rather
than balanced.

First, traditional models in developmental psychology
(particularly in child development) have placed primary
emphasis on intraorganismic sources or mechanisms of developmental change in contrast to external, contextual influences.
In infancy and early childhood, neurophysiological and maturational variables have been considered the key developmental
antecedents of most types of behavioral change. For example,
the parallel between maturational factors and the child's
physical development (Gesell, 1940) was assumed to hold also
for the relationship between neurophysiological development
and cognitive functioning. Such assumed linkage between intraorganismic, maturational variables and behavioral development is reflected in writings, such as Gesell and Ilg (1943),
which describe the characteristic development of the child
with little reference to external, environmental influences.

Secondly, emphasis has been place on normative, universal
patterns of development (influenced largely by genetic, maturational factors) in contrast to individual differences in
development. This normative developmental approach is illustrated in cross-cultural Piagetian research on cognitive functioning (Goodnow, 1962), where the concern has been for replication of universal stage sequences rather than for exploring
how various cultures differentially affected the timing and
behavioral manifestation of cognitive functioning. This pre-
dominant emphasis on intraorganismic, personological and normative factors is also found in the study of later adulthood.
It has been widely held that the nature of intellectual decline in aging is rather universal (across abilities and persons). Moreover, until recently, potential decline in intellectual performance in old age has been primarily attributed
to biological factors rather than to the possible negative
cumulation of environmental life events and the effects of a
deprived environment (Labouvie, Hoyer, Baltes, & Baltes,
1974).

Finally, personological models have characterized development as occurring in a static cultural context with little
attention to macro-level cultural change. Even when persono-

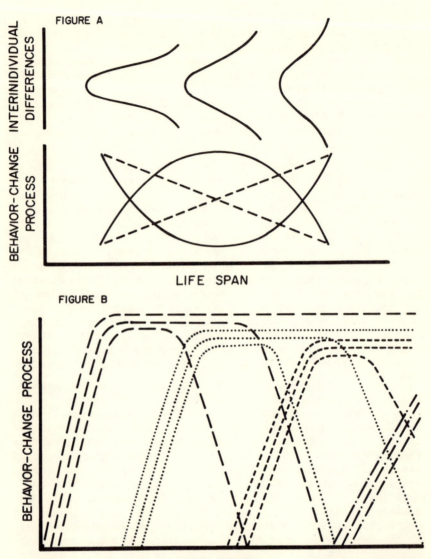

Figure 1. Selective examples of life-span developmental processes: Figure 1A illustrates multidimensionality, multidirectionality, and age-correlated increases in interindividual variability. Figure 1B summarizes notions of life-course grading and discontinuity. Developmental functions (behavior-change processes) differ in terms of onset, duration, and termination when charted in the framework of the life course; moreover, they involve both quantitative and qualitative aspects of change (from Baltes, Cornelius, & Nesselroade, 1979, in press ©Academic Press).

logical models of development have made explicit the role of
environmental socialization factors, most developmental
psychologists have behaved as if this context were fairly
invariant with all individuals participating (throughout
ontogeny) in a prescribed and fairly universal age-related
sequence of socialization events. This normative socialization sequence was seen (often in conjunction with a convergent process of normative biological maturation) as producing regularities in ontogenetic development. Indeed, one
of the outcomes for developmental psychologists of the
1960's war on poverty and the resulting compensatory education programs was the heightened awareness of the culturally
different child and variability in behavioral development
(Sigel & Brodzinsky, 1977).

For someone outside the mainstream of developmental psychology, the relative neglect of cultural factors and of the
importance of biocultural change in traditional developmental
psychology might be surprising. In our view, however, this
characterization of the field is an accurate representation of
its dominant themes, some vigorous exceptions (e.g., Committee
on Human Development, 1965; LeVine, 1970) notwithstanding.

Search for New Conceptions of Development

The emergence of a life-span developmental perspective,
then, is beginning to contribute to an expansion and reformu-
lation of existing conceptions of behavioral development. On
a general level, this applies to both the descriptive and to
the explanatory-analytic efforts in developmental work. Figures 1 and 2 are illustrative of this search for new conceptions of development. In a later section, the area of intellectual behavior will be examined to provide a concrete research example.

1. **Multidimensionality, Multidirectionality, and Life-
course Grading.** On the level of identifying ontogenetic
change, Figure 1 (A & B) summarizes evolving conceptions of
development which stem largely from a life-span approach. In
fact, the first American textbook on life-span developmental
psychology (Hollingworth, 1927) already contains the foundations for the perspective represented in Figure 1.

In the past (e.g., Harris, 1957), the central approach to
defining development in the context of child psychology was to
view it as a fairly unitary process. Following the guidelines
provided by philosophers and especially biologists, development was defined as a behavior-change process with specific
progression-related characteristics. The salient features of
such a "developmental" behavior-change process were that the
change was unidirectional, sequential, qualitative, irreversi-

ble, fairly normative (across persons and behaviors), and oriented towards an endstate (e.g., maturity). Such a concept of development is closely related to the biologist's concept of growth. A large number of features had to be met for a behavior-change process to be called developmental. This is why this biology-oriented concept of development is occasionally labelled a "strong" concept of development. More recently, articles by Wohlwill (1970) and McCall (1977) continue in that tradition, though largely in the context of child development. Similarly, chapters by Reese and Overton (Reese & Overton, 1970; Overton & Reese, 1973) are helpful in articulating the unique metatheoretical features which different concepts of development display. These chapters distinguish between organismic and mechanistic concepts of development. Organismic conceptions, both on the level of the description and explanation, are part of the class of concepts of development which we have labelled "strong."

Life-span researchers have begun to view this particular conception of development as being unduly restrictive and as only one type of case among a larger array of possibilities. Figure 1 represents some alternatives. The central themes depicted in Figure 1 are that, in a life-span developmental framework, developmental functions can display multiple directions, diverse trajectories, and much interindividual variability and intraindividual plasticity.

Specifically, Figure 1A focuses on increasing interindividual variability in behavior as the life-course evolves (upper part) and, on multidimensionality and multidirectionality (lower part of figure). These features add up to a concern with differential processes of development. Differential development is used here to indicate that the forms of developmental change are not unitary. Rather, such change displays much diversity on the intraindividual level (across situations and behaviors) as well as on the level of interindividual differences (both within and between cohorts).

Figure 1B supplements the general approach outlined in Figure 1A. It adds to the notions of multidimensionality, multidirectionality, and plasticity (or intra- and interindividual variability) conceptions of life-course grading and discontinuity. Following Neugarten's (1969, see also Neugarten & Hagestad, 1976) earlier suggestions, discontinuity and life-course grading point to two salient features of life-span development. First, the terms suggest that behavior-change processes do not necessarily represent change as a simple cumulation along an invariant continuum of measurement. Second, not all behavior-change processes extend across the entire life span. They do not all originate at birth and terminate

at death. The central notion expressed in Figure 1B is that
the life-course of individuals evidences patterns of multiple
behavior-change processes which differ not only in direction-
ality but also in ages of onset, duration, and termination.

Thus, life-span developmental psychologists, while ac-
knowledging the usefulness of a biologically-oriented growth
concept as one type of developmental change, are much impress-
ed with the substantial magnitude of diversity and discontinuity which ontogenetic development seems to display (e.g.,
Huston-Stein & Baltes, 1976; Hollingworth, 1927; Neugarten,
1969). It is as yet open to question how far such a plural-
istic view can be pushed without risking loss of the unique
strength of a developmental approach. However, it is evident
that simple, unitary, and cumulative conceptions of development are insufficient when it comes to the task of charting
processes of life-span development.

2. Multiple and Interacting Sources of Development. The
previous section and Figure 1 dealt with description of developmental change. Figure 2 focuses on explanatory factors and
principles to account for the complexity of the life-span
changes summarized in the previous section. This figure com-
bines Riley's (Riley et al., 1972; Riley, 1976) sociological
model of aging and cohort flow with perspectives provided by
life-span developmental psychology (Baltes, 1976; 1979, in
press; Baltes, Cornelius, & Nesselroade, 1979, in press).

The scheme represented in Figure 2 attempts to delineate
major antecedent systems influencing individual development,
and to summarize general principles of theory building. The
center upper part of the figure identifies three major systems
of influences on development. They are: ontogenetic age-
graded, evolutionary history-graded, and non-normative. These
influence systems interact in the production of developmental
behavior-change processes. However, it must be recognized at
the outset that the definition of these age-graded, history-
graded, and non-normative influences is not simple, nor do
these influences necessarily fall into three distinct unre-
lated classes. Moreover, it is likely that their definition
varies among researchers, particularly if oriented to different disciplines. Thus, the present effort is prototheoretical
and heuristic only.

Age-graded influences refer to biological and environmental determinants which exhibit a high degree of correlation
with chronological age. They follow from the traditional
focus on biological maturation and, as to socialization, from
viewing the life-course as consisting of a series of normative
age-graded (Neugarten & Hagestad, 1976) tasks and socializa-

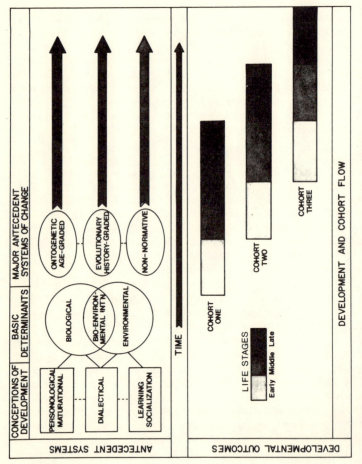

Figure 2. Illustration of relationship among life-span development, cohorts, and three major influence systems: ontogentic (age-graded), evolutionary (history-graded), and non-normative (non-
developmental). The figure is taken from Baltes, Cornelius, and Nesselroade (1979 © Academic Press).
The lower part of the figure is an adaptation of the model of aging and cohort flow present by
Riley (e.g., Riley et al., 1972).

tion influences. <u>History-graded</u> influences are those fairly normative-universal event patterns which occur in connection with biosocial change as evidenced, for example, in cohort effects. They exhibit a high correlation with historical time and apply to most individuals of a given cultural unit. Non-<u>normative</u> influences, finally, are those which are significant in their effect on development but are not normative in the sense that they do not occur for everyone or not necessarily in easily discernible and invariant sequences or patterns through the life-course of individuals.

As to non-normative influences, Dohrenwend and Dohren-wend's (1974) concept of critical life events (see also Hultsch & Plemons, 1979, in press) is a good example. There appear to be two major subclasses of non-normative influences. The first is related to historical time and deals with event patterns at the macrolevel such as wars, economic depression, or health epidemics which are not universal but specific to historical moments, regions, and clusters of people. The second subclass parallels age-graded influences and involves significant life events (illness, loss of employment, divorce, death of significant others) at the individual level. The assumption is that unique combinations and sequences of such non-normative influences represent a substantial part of the influences operating in the production of life-span changes in behavior.

Figure 2 suggests also that some of these distinct in-fluence systems can be seen as having primary origins in one of the dominant models within developmental psychology: ma-turational, dialectical, and learning-socialization. However, it would be superficial to link them to any of these models in a unitary fashion. This is particularly true because all in-fluence systems, in principle, involve both environmental and biological determinants and mechanisms (see also Lerner, 1976). Dotted lines connecting the three influence systems (other connections could be added) suggest that they interact with each other, and arrows to the right along the time continuum indicate that the influence systems accumulate in their ef-fects and change with time. Note also that the distinction of the influences provided by the three influence systems is not always convergent, neither in timing nor in strength. Thus, as Riegel (1977) discussed in the context of ontogeny, it is necessary to examine carefully the extent of synchronicity and colinearity which age-graded, history-graded, and non-norma-tive influences display as the life-course of a given cohort unfolds.

The lower part of Figure 2 is designed to illustrate how successive cohorts of individuals develop at different epochs

and in the context of different cohort combinations. Therefore, in their life-course, successive cohorts may respond to
and interact with different patterns of factors associated
with the three classes of influence systems outlined in the
upper part of the figure. This part of the figure is taken
from the work of Riley and her colleagues (Riley et al., 1972)
in sociology.

A final observation on the relationship between Figures
1 and 2: Figure 1 emphasized the need for multidimensionality,
multidirectionality, and plasticity in representing the complexity of life-span development on the descriptive level.
Figure 2 emphasizes the existence of distinct explanatory sets
of influences (age-graded, history-graded, non-normative)
which are themselves changing with time. It is important to
recognize that there is a high degree of conceptual convergence between descriptive efforts (Figure 1) and explanatory
(Figure 2) efforts. This is so because diversity in influences (nature, patterning, sequencing, duration, etc.) is a
prerequisite for diversity in developmental outcomes. In this
sense, both figures supplement each other in the search for
comprehensive views of development as suggested by a life-span
developmental psychology.

<u>Psychometric Intelligence
and Life-Span Development</u>

This next section will illustrate in the area of psychometric intelligence, why a life-span approach has generated
the types of theoretical perspectives summarized in Figure 1
and 2. This presentation is necessarily selective and largely
a condensation of ideas contained in recent writings by Baltes, Labouvie-Vief, Schaie, and their colleagues (e.g., Baltes
& Labouvie, 1973; Baltes & Schaie, 1976; Labouvie-Vief &
Chandler, 1978; Riegel, 1973; Schaie, 1977, 1979, in press;
Schaie & Baltes, 1977). It should also be acknowledged that
not all researchers necessarily agree with all of the themes
presented here (as in writings by Horn, 1978; Horn & Donaldson, 1976; and Botwinick, 1977).

<u>Multidimensionality</u>, <u>Multidirectionality</u>, and <u>Variability</u>

Descriptive evidence on multidimensionality and multidirectionality of psychometric intelligence is widely accepted.
Following Cattell's (1971) lead, Horn's (1970, 1978) reviews
are perhaps most comprehensive and consistent in their conclusion that psychometric intelligence is not a unitary dimension but a multidimensional construct involving distinct
classes of intellectual behavior. In addition to the Horn-
Cattell theory of fluid-crystallized intelligence, Thurstone's

or Guilford's structure-of-intellect models, each involving a
multitude of dimensions, are widely known examples.

Horn and Cattell have also been most explicit (though
sometimes without adequate empirical support) in adding to the
notion of multidimensionality that of multidirectionality. In
other words, the intellectual behavior of a multitude of
people in a diverse set of contexts not only exhibits a multidimensional pattern of intellectual abilities (factors, dimensions). In addition, when one considers the course of life-
span development, these multiple abilities can each exhibit
distinct developmental curves or functions. For example, as
most persuasively argued by Horn (1970, 1978), fluid intelligence tends to exhibit an inverted U-shaped function through
the life-span, with maximum performance for most people around
the completion of the third decade of life. Crystallized
intelligence, by contrast, is assumed to display a developmental function exhibiting progression or maintenance of
performance up until late adulthood.

Thus, the Horn-Cattell theory of psychometric intelligence
is not in line with some of the traditional features of development conceived as a unitary progression, but focuses on
multidimensionality and multidirectionality. In terms of
empirical data base, Schaie's cohort-sequential work (Schaie,
1970, 1978) is clearly the most persuasive on these points.
Using Thurstone's model of primary mental abilities, Schaie
and his colleagues have been able to show dramatic differences
in the level and direction of adult-developmental changes.
This was true both for classes of intellectual behavior (e.g.,
psychomotor speed vs. vocabulary) and for distinct age-cohorts.
As a consequence, in the area of life-span psychometric intelligence, the case for a multidimensional and multidirectional
conception has been set forth.

The case seems also to have been made on the issue of interindividual variability and intraindividual plasticity.
While Horn (1970, 1978) and Botwinick (1977) continue to
focus on normative change functions (across persons and cohorts), there is mounting evidence of much variability and
plasticity associated with distinct historical contexts and
life-course experiences. This evidence comes from two lines
of research, the first involving comparative work with criterion groups, the second involving the consequences of direct
intervention work. Illustrative examples for the first line
of research are work on cohort effects (see Baltes, Cornelius,
& Nesselroade, 1978 for review), which suggests variability
among birth-cohorts in the course of intellectual development;
research on the impact of professional career environments on
adult intelligence (e.g., Kohn & Schooler, 1977, and their

chapter in this volume); evidence on the impact of educational differences on the nature of intellectual functioning in advanced adulthood (e.g., Gardner & Monge, 1978); or findings on large interindividual differences at given age levels in the latter part of the life course (e.g., Schaie & Parham, 1977).

The second line of research on variability is aimed directly at studying the conditions under which the same individuals, as they age, exhibit different levels and forms of intellectual behavior. This research is manipulative-interventive and focuses on intraindividual functioning.

A central example of this approach has been the use of practice (training) and other performance-related support systems (e.g., motivation, cautiousness) for exploring the range of intraindividual variability (plasticity) in intellectual performance in older adults. Such intervention research has produced rather dramatic increases and decreases in old people's intellectual performance (see Baltes & Baltes, 1977; Labouvie-Vief, 1976 for reviews). For example, Plemons, Willis, & Baltes (1977) were recently able to show in older persons (age range 59-85) that eight one-hour training sessions dealing with one component of fluid intelligence ("figural relations") resulted in marked improvement and also in some generalization to other intellectual tests used to assess transfer of training to other domains of intelligence. This transfer of training effect was maintained at a follow-up evaluation obtained six months after training. Furthermore, older persons have consistently evidenced marked retest gains of the general performance kind when they were asked to participate repeatedly in the taking of intelligence tests. Even such behavior of older persons as response speed (often related to a decline in neurophysiological functioning) has been demonstrated to be somewhat modifiable in older persons by means of practice and reinforcement contingencies (e.g., Hoyer, Labouvie & Baltes, 1973). As a consequence, it seems fair to conclude that there is much plasticity in intellectual behavior of the aged. Thus, it is reasonable to infer that the course of intellectual aging is highly modifiable, dependent to a large degree on the nature of the support (or deficit of support) in the old person's concurrent and past environments.

It is not yet clear how far the question of ontogenetic transformation and plasticity in intelligence can be pushed. In fact, it is important to understand that we cannot postulate a complete absence of normative developmental trends if we are to maintain a developmental approach as a useful theoretical and methodological perspective (McCall, 1977; Wohlwill,

1973). Thus, while it is demonstrated that there is multi-dimensionality, multidirectionality, interindividual variability, and intraindividual plasticity in ontogeny on the level of <u>quantitative</u> analysis (how much? what direction?), it is not clear whether there are counterpart <u>qualitative</u> differences in structure and processing. The question of qualitative differences relates to the notions of discontinuity and life-course grading illustrated in the preceeding Figure 1B. On the one hand, there is much evidence for the early life-span that there is little predictability from early to adult life in psychometric intelligence (Horn, 1978). On the other hand, Schaie's data on adult and gerontological intelligence for the life-course show a picture of much higher stability in interindividual differences and, therefore, much higher predictability than is true for childhood. The major problem is that, for the most part, we have not yet addressed the question of suitable or unique tasks for measuring "gerontological" or late-life cognition. Notable exceptions include preliminary work by Clayton (1980, in press) on wisdom, by Gardner and Monge (1977) on adult-relevant tests, by Riegel (1973) on a fifth stage of Piagetian operations, and by Schaie (1977) who offers prototheoretical suggestions on adult cognitive stages.

In sum, the evidence accumulated thus far is sufficiently strong to mandate a search for alternative conceptions of adult psychometric intelligence (see also, Labouvie-Vief, 1977). And, the evidence is in convergence with the general theoretical perspectives expressed in Figure 1 above, which expands the traditional concept of development beyond that of a normative and unidirectional process to include behavior-change processes having features of multidimensionality, multidirectionality, and large inter- as well as intraindividual variability (plasticity).

Multiple Sources of Influences

As we turn now to the effect of explanatory determinants and the role of multiple systems of influences (represented in Figure 2 above) the data base is so far less rich, but nonetheless consistent.

1. <u>Age-graded Influences</u>. The effect of age-graded influences on life-span intelligence is perhaps best reflected in research on childhood and adolescent intelligence. For the most part, such research has emphasized a conjoint unfolding operation of maturational and socialization processes. A very clear-cut expression of such an age-graded approach is inherent in the formal educational system. In a more general context, Parelius (1975) discusses numerous ex-

amples of how current educational scheduling leads to various
forms of age-stratification throughout life.

What is most relevant for the present context is that it
is less clear which age-related life course variables operate
on psychometric intelligence in any consistent manner following early adulthood. While educational and maturational
schedules correlate highly with chronological age up to adolescence, subsequent age-correlated schedules are less conspicuous. This is likely also the primary reason why chronological age appears to lose much of its power as an organizing
search variable as one moves into adulthood and old age, at
least in the area of psychometric intelligence. If one
follows Schaie's (Schaie & Parham, 1977) recent reanalysis of
his cohort-sequential data, it is not until the late seventh
and eighth decade of human life that age-correlated determinants recapture a dominant position in the explanation of
intellectual variance and the course of intellectual aging.

What then are the primary guiding factors in adult development of psychometric intelligence? In our view, these are
increasingly related to the operation of history-graded and
non-normative influences as described in Figure 2. To begin
with, it is reasonable to assume that early life, age-correlated factors such as education will continue to have a long-
term effect, particularly as they mediate subsequent professional career trajectories (e.g., Kohn & Schooler, 1977).
Indeed, educational level accounts for a large share of interindividual differences in the intellectual performance of
older adults (Schaie & Willis, 1978). Furthermore, as mentioned above, it is quite possible that, following a life-
course grading model, there are unique cognitive tasks in late
life. These might either stimulate the acquisition of new
cognitive skills, or result in the extinction or transformation of skills which are losing their adaptiveness in old age.

2. History-graded Influences. The impact of history-
graded influences is best illustrated by research on cohort
differences in adult development, most notably the work of
Schaie. Schaie's (1970, 1979, in press) cohort-sequential
project on adult intelligence (as noted above) involved the
longitudinal study of a large number of subjects from the
adult age range (24 to 80 years old). He observed each of a
number of age samples stemming from different cohorts three
times over a 14-year period (in 1956, 1963, and 1970). Dependent measures were intelligence tests from the Primary
Mental Abilities (Thurstone) and Schaie's Test of Behavioral
Rigidity. The design permitted the plotting of 14-year change
data, for each of 7 separate age/cohorts: for example, from
age 24 to 38, 31 to 45, 38 to 52, 45 to 59, 52 to 66, 59 to

73, and 66 to 80.

The key findings shatter any theory of adult intelligence which is based on universal and normative developmental trends such as aging decline. Instead, the outcome showed a picture of very strong cohort differences associated with social-change effects. In fact, the magnitude of cohort differences was, in general, larger than age changes within cohorts, at least up to the seventh decade of life. For example, different cohorts aged very differently in intelligence; thus persons of the same age (e.g., 60-year-olds, in 1956 vs. 1963 vs. 1970), but from different birth cohorts, exhibited rather discrepant quantitative change patterns ranging from increments to stability to decrements. Moreover, Schaie's data produced very little evidence of any universal decline in intelligence (across persons and distinct dimensions of intellectual performance). Some cohorts on some dimensions of intelligence (e.g., crystallized) showed increments, let's say from age 45 to 52, while the same cohorts evidenced decline on others (e.g., fluid intelligence). To put the same findings a different way, the different historical periods (1956 to 1963 vs. 1963 to 1970, etc.) produced quite discrepant outcomes in the nature of quantitative intellectual aging for identical age groups drawn from different birth-cohorts.

While Schaie's research is the most comprehensive on the impact of historical change on life-span development of psychometric intelligence, there are many corroborative findings in related domains of behavior and for other segments of the life span (see Baltes et al., 1978, for review). Zajonc (1976), for example, has attempted to formulate a family constellation-based model in an effort to account for the well known cohort-related declines in adolescent performance on the Scholastic Aptitude Test.

Another example comes from research on neonatal behavior. There is a hotly debated issue in that field on the question of whether or not neonates can be classically conditioned. The last 20 years have seen many conflicting data and confusing arguments. In 1976, Porges examined these data from a social change or cohort perspective, looking at historical changes in the life space of infants, as in procedures of pre-, co-, and postnatal medical practices surrounding birth. Porges reached the conclusion that the last 20 to 30 years have seen major changes in such practices dealing, for example, with medication and maternal nutrition during pregnancy, birth, and the postpartum period. Having demonstrated this, Porges (1976) proceeded to argue that such historical changes in the medical conditions surrounding pregnancy and birth have presented researchers with

quite different types of infant organisms at distinct historical periods, different at least for the first 1 to 4
days of life. Depending on the medical practices affecting
particular cohorts, the infants' activity levels are different, as are their capabilities to attend. Accordingly, Porges argues that the questions of whether neonates can or cannot be classically conditioned cannot be answered with a
strict personological and history-free approach. One needs
to consider the biocultural context in which infants "trans-
act"; so the question of conditionability becomes one of contingencies. Moreover, Porges argued that such a contextual-
interactive position suggests that any developmental finding
collected at a particular historical point is likely to be
but a sample from a larger population of possible findings.

Finally, a study by Nesselroade and Baltes (1974) can
serve to illustrate further the role of history-graded influences. They examined via a cohort-sequential, longitudinal
design approximately 2,000 West Virginia adolescents (age
range 13 to 17) in 1970, 1971, and 1972. Using both personality and ability measures as dependent variables, they found
that, in the case of personality, the historical moment (1970
vs. 1971 vs. 1972) rather than chronological age (from 13 to
14 to 15 to 16) was the more powerful factor in accounting for
the course of adolescent personality development. Specifically, regardless of their age, over the two-year period from
1970 to 1972, adolescents developed in the direction of less
super-ego strength, less achievement orientation, and more
independence and autonomy.

3. Non-normative Life Events. As mentioned in describing Figure 2, the three postulated influence systems are not
necessarily mutually exclusive and, in addition, their deline-
ation is preliminary and might differ depending upon one's
conceptual orientation. The difficulties of distinct definition are particularly conspicuous in the case of non-normative
life events. In principle, since time is necessarily involved
when determinants operate in concrete situations, non-normative events will always exhibit a degree of correlation with
age- and history-graded processes. The major characteristic
of these non-normative events is that they show little consistent normalization in onset, duration, or sequencing for
different persons and different domains of behavior.

In the area of psychometric intelligence, there is only
beginning evidence for the operation of non-normative events;
at least, the existing evidence has not yet been brought together in any systematic manner. Father absence, for example,
has been linked to lowered scholastic achievement, particularly for boys. Santrock (1972) found that effects of father

absence (because of divorce, separation, or desertion) during
early childhood were more devastating to scholastic performance of lower class 3rd and 6th grade children than to performance of older children. Shelton (1969) also has reported
that father-absent boys compared with father-present boys in
junior high school made lower grades in both academic and non-
academic subjects. In the gerontological literature, an
example for non-normative factors is Botwinick's (1967) conception of modifiers of intellectual performance, such as the
role of illness, occupation, or leisure life. As another
example, specific illness-related physical disabilities may
also be linked to intellectual functioning. Thus, in both
young populations (Hine, 1970) and older populations (Granick,
Kleban, & Weiss, 1976) hearing loss has been found to be related to reductions in cognitive functioning.

Many such non-normative factors of associated processes
might be important in determining the course of life-span intelligence. Their occurence, however, is not universal nor,
if they do occur, do they exhibit universal patterns of onset,
duration, constellation, or sequencing. Yet, despite the
paucity of relevant empirical data, we believe that the systematic examination of such non-normative life events will
provide a powerful avenue towards the understanding of adult
intelligence, especially in terms of quantitative changes and
the large interindividual variability and variations in tra-
jectory.

4. Interactions. Examination of the interactions among
the three sources of influences listed is the least advanced
area of research, in part because appropriate methodological
strategies are only recently being formulated.

Thus in the area of life-span intelligence, the current
scene is primarily one of conceptual model building. However,
as illustrated in the lower part of Figure 2 and in Riley's
models of the interplay between aging and social change (see
her chapters in this book), a conceptual case can easily be
made for the likelihood of interactive formulations involving
age-graded, history-graded, and non-normative life events. In
the psychological literature, Riegel's (1976, 1977) discussion
of dialectical conceptions of aging is rich in such suggestions. Similarly, Uhlenberg's chapter in this book shows the
changing nature of old age in the United States from a sociological point of view as resulting from interactions between
distinct ontogenetic and historical sets of influences.
Furthermore, forecasting the future of aging patterns as conducted by futurists (see Gordon's chapter in this book) also
involves consideration of differential ontogenetic-historical
interaction patterns across time.

Life-Span Development
and Social Policy

Social policy affords one form of intervention into the course of life-span development and aging. Social policy and intervention both imply a plan for arranging conditions under which particular behavioral and societal outcomes are prevented, achieved, or maintained. Of course, knowledge about the course and conditions of psychological human development represents only one important facet to be considered in formulating social policy.

What are some of the implications of a life-span developmental approach for the formulation of social policy, using the area of education as an example? The new catch words suggested by a life-span orientation are: multidirectionality, multidimensionality, large interindividual differences, and modifiability or plasticity, all conceptualized in an interactive contextual framework. This view results in a conception of behavior development which is a "differential developmental psychology."

In fact, some researchers argue that what we observe when studying "naturally occurring" psychological development is but a small segment of what psychological development could be like if the social, environmental, and biological support context were engineered to be different. Such a difference- and plasticity-oriented view is particularly appropriate for the second part of the human life-span.

Life-Span Social Policy

Since we suggest a direct linkage between the basic tenets of a life-span approach and conceptions of social policy, the following generic principles should hold.

First, it follows that social policy should involve a life-span perspective as well. An age-segmented approach to social policy involves many of the same limitations as found in age-specific psychological models of development. Social intervention into one age period must be preceded by an examination of possible side effects for other age periods and by designing a policy which considers interage linkages.

Second, a life-span social policy needs to focus on preventative optimization and not only on alleviation. In the case of aging, this suggestion implies that the focus for intervention is not necessarily the aged. On the contrary, in line with the assumption that aging is a life-long process, much of social policy needs to deal with younger age groups.

Such a preventative orientation toward the future might detract from the current needs of the aged. At the same time, it appears reasonable to argue that (particularly when age-graded influences are involved) a life-span distribution of social policy efforts is the only strategy which, in the long run, is capable of using resources in an optimal manner by dealing with problems before they occur or even by preventing their occurrence.

Third, because of the pervasiveness of differential development, social policy needs to be differential social policy. Life-span changes involve increasing variability, with chronological age becoming less and less relevant as we move towards adulthood and old age. This is largely true because there is less age-graded socialization in the second part of life(see also Rosow, 1971) and because history-graded and non-normative events gain in prominence. Accordingly, social policy for the second part of life cannot be normative; it needs to be flexible and differential. Such a call for a differential social policy is also supported by the notion of intraindividual plasticity. Aging individuals need to be able to continue to maximize their human potential in a context which is supportive of independent and often idiosyncratic functioning and the view that important developmental tasks continue to unfold.

Fourth, a life-span developmental orientation suggests a cultural-change conscious social policy. Different combinations of age-graded, history-graded and non-normative influences operate to produce distinct developmental outcomes for different cohorts. The implication for social policy is that such developmental change would require new and different social policies, always formulated, however, in an overarching framework of cohort-sequential life-course trajectories. Publications by Neugarten and Havighurst (1976, 1977) are illustrative of such a cultural-change conscious approach to social policy and social ethics as it applies to current and future aging cohorts.

Life-Span Education

The general themes of a life-span, preventative-optimization, differential, and cultural change-consciousness approach to social policy are easily applied to the area of education. Currently, educational services are heavily concentrated in the periods of early life (childhood, adolescence). Thus, the primary guidelines for the format of current education are developed within a frame of reference that owes much to the kind of child-development conception presented earlier with little concern for life-span development (Dave, 1976; Dave &

Lengrand, 1974; Montada & Filipp, 1976).

For example, the posture of life-long differential development and the view of plasticity would suggest a strong case for redistributing education across the life-span (see also Birren & Woodruff, 1973; Riley, Johnson, & Foner, 1972; Schaie & Willis, 1978). The implied assumption is that education, concentrated in early life, cannot prepare the individual for a life-time of ontogenetic changes resulting from novel combinations of age-graded, history-graded, and non-normative influences. In this vein, Montada and Filipp (1976) have argued that the content of childhood education efforts cannot be guided only by childhood and status quo orientations; it must include the teaching of preventative life-skill techniques which facilitate adjustment in late life and in a changing society. Similarly, Dubin (1974), in a review article on occupational obsolescence and life-long learning, asserted that a major portion of the educational system should be devoted to preventative updating in light of a changing cultural context, rather than massed education in early life for the rest of life. Such a demand for life-long education is not only supported by the conclusion that the second part of life contains novel tasks to be mastered by the individual (Schaie & Quayhagen, 1978; Havighurst, 1972), but also by requirements of teaching technology. Learning principles suggest that a contextual subject matter-specific component is important in designing for optimal learning (Gagne, 1968; Wroczynski, 1974). The child or young adult, however, has not yet had many of the relevant life experiences which provide a useful context for facilitating the learning of certain subject matter or life skills (Brim & Wheeler, 1966; Cropley, 1976; Houle, 1974; Riley, Foner, Hess, & Toby, 1969) requisite for effective adaptation in advanced stages of the life course.

The general demand for life-long education is, of course, not new (Yeaxlee, 1929). Adult education and continuing education endeavors have frequently used the term "life span" to suggest expansion of traditional education into the adult period. However, what is unique to the current life-span approach is the formulation of a set of generic developmental principles. The salient general propositions are, as was true for social policy, life-span education, differential education, preventative-optimizing education, and cultural change-conscious education.

As to life-span education, the recommendation is to distribute educational resources throughout the life course. The assumption is that since there is ontogenetic-developmental change across the entire life span, educational inter-

vention must also be life long in nature in order to optimize
and facilitate development. However, it is important to view
life-span education not simply as a continuous cumulation and
extension of childhood-education and higher education models,
neither in technology, format, nor subject matter (Schaie &
Willis, 1978). A life-span approach suggests both continuity
and discontinuity in development. Therefore, it is important
to consider both continuous and discontinuous developmental
tasks and conditions associated with the life course as summarized in Figures 1 and 2. Unique developmental tasks at
each stage in the life span must be incorporated into educational intervention. At the same time, consideration of the
prior developmental and educational history of the individual
is useful in designing concurrent intervention endeavors.

The concept of differential education is important because life-span development becomes less normative and less
homogeneous with increasing age. Thus, as life-span development is highly differential, educational systems will need to
show a counterpart high level of differentiation both in terms
of the substance of education and timing. Such differentiation will allow for multiple and discontinuous educational
pathways for different individuals and subgroups of persons.
Furthermore, the concept of what constitutes education (substance, format, etc.) will need to be either re-evaluated,
expanded, or subsumed under a more general concept such as
human development intervention. Moreover, because not all
educational needs can be predicted with sufficient accuracy
(e.g., those due to non-normative events), the concept of
differential education also implies that educational entry and
exit opportunities need to be made as flexible as possible
(Dave, 1976).

With regard to the principle of preventative optimization
in educational policies, the task is one of arranging for
educational systems which not only anticipate the course of
human development, but also contain conditions facilitative of
progressive mastery of subsequent components of the developmental course. In fact, it is knowledge about the course and
mechanisms of life-span development which provides the strength
of a developmental approach to intervention including education (Baltes & Danish, 1978; Birren & Woodruff, 1973; Cropley,
1976; Urban, 1976). The life-span conceptions outlined in
Figures 1 and 2, however, make it also clear why it is unlikely that all aspects of life-span development can be adequately addressed with a preventative-optimizing strategy.
Those processes and problems which are primarily related to
history-graded and non-normative influences cannot be fully
predicted. In spite of such non-normative developmental influences, it may be possible to maintain some form of preven-

tion-optimization strategies nevertheless. For example, mechanisms for ad hoc educational planning need to be made available, if the need should arise. Similarly, to the end of dealing with non-normative life events, the Hamburgs, Danish, and their colleagues (e.g., Coelho, Hamburg, & Adams, 1974; Danish, 1977) have begun to develop educational intervention models which are aimed at enhancing general life or coping skills. These skills are assumed to be relevant in a large array of potential life tasks or crises and, therefore, assumed to exhibit preventative-optimizing potential even for non-normative situations.

The principle of <u>cultural</u> change <u>consciousness</u> in <u>educa-tional policies</u> is perhaps the least articulated. Concepts such as educational obsolescence and continuing education (Dave, 1976; Hiemstra, 1976) have been introduced to acknowl-edge the possibility of maintaining educational efforts throughout life. Their rationale has been developed, however, largely in the context of occupational careers (Dubin, 1972, 1974). Comparatively little attention has been paid to multi-faceted requirements and educational targets as implied, for example, in Toffler's (1970) <u>Future</u> <u>Shock</u>. Thus, it is our impression that this feature of life-span educational policy, while evident on the conceptual level, is the one deserving most vigorous thought at this moment in time. The rate of cultural change appears to be so high that education for the status quo is only a part of what is necessary for individuals to be able to master and contribute to the future as their life development progresses.

The prototheoretical notions of differential development and intellectual plasticity inherent in current life-span thinking, however, provide useful generic principles when considering cultural change issues. This foundation is apt to generate optimism about what could be accomplished if we ac-cept the challenge of a cultural change-conscious approach to life-span education. Such an orientation suggests the need for dynamic educational policies which are not only reactive to cultural change, but also assertively involved in deter-mining the direction of some aspects of its future course.

References

Baltes, M. M., & Baltes, P. B. The ecopsychological rela-
    tivity and plasticity of psychological aging: Conver-
    gent perspectives of cohort effects and operant psychol-
    ogy. <u>Zeitschrift</u> <u>fur</u> <u>Experimentelle</u> <u>und</u> <u>Angewandte</u>
    <u>Psychologie</u>, 1977, <u>24</u>, 179-197.

Baltes, P. B. (Chm). Symposium: Life-span developmental psychology: Implications for child development. In H. W. Reese (Ed.), Advances in child development and behavior (Vol. 11). New York: Academic Press, 1976.

Baltes, P. B. Life-span developmental psychology: Observations on history and theory. In P. B. Baltes & O. G. Brim, Jr. (Eds.), Life-span development and behavior (Vol. 2). New York: Academic Press, 1979, in press.

Baltes, P. B., Cornelius, S. W., & Nesselroade, J. R. Cohort effects in behavioral development: Theoretical and methodological perspectives. In W. A. Collins (Ed.), Minnesota symposium on child psychology (Vol. 11). Hillsdale: Erlbaum, 1978, in press.

Baltes, P. B., Cornelius, S. W., & Nesselroade, J. R. Cohort effects in developmental psychology. In J. R. Nesselroade & P. B. Baltes (Eds.), Longitudinal research in human development: Design and analysis. New York: Academic Press, 1979, in press.

Baltes, P. B., & Danish, S. J. Intervention in life-span development and aging: Issues and concepts. Zeitschrift für Entwicklungspsychologie und Pädagogische Psychologie, 1978, in press.

Baltes, P. B., & Labouvie, G. V. Adult development of intellectual performance: Description, explanation, and modification. In C. Eisdorfer & M. P. Lawton (Eds.), The psychology of adult development and aging. Washington, D.C.: American Psychological Association, 1973.

Baltes, P. B., & Schaie, K. W. (Eds.). Life-span developmental psychology: Personality and socialization. New York: Academic Press, 1973.

Baltes, P. B., & Schaie, K. W. On the plasticity of intelligence in adulthood and old age: Where Horn and Donaldson fail. American Psychologist, 1976, 31, 720-725.

Birren, J. E., & Woodruff, D. Human development over the life-span through education. In P. B. Baltes & K. W. Schaie (Eds.), Life-span developmental psychology: Personality and socialization. New York: Academic Press, 1973.

Botwinick, J. Cognitive processes in maturity and old age. New York: Springer, 1967.

Botwinick, J. Aging and intelligence. In J. E. Birren & K. W. Schaie (Eds.), Handbook of the psychology of aging.

New York: Van Nostrand-Reinhold, 1977.

Brim, O. G., & Wheeler, S. Socialization after childhood: Two essays. New York: Wiley, 1966.

Bronfenbrenner, U. Toward an experimental ecology of human development. American Psychologist, 1977, 32, 513-531.

Cattell, R. B. Abilities: Their structure, growth, and action. Boston: Houghton, 1971.

Clayton, V. Age and wisdom across the life-span: Theoretical perspectives. In P. B. Baltes & O. G. Brim, Jr. (Eds.), Life-span development and behavior (Vol. 3). New York: Academic Press, 1980, in preparation.

Coehlho, G. V., Hamburg, D. A., & Adams, J. E. (Eds). Coping and adaptation. New York: Basic Books, 1974.

Committee on Human Development (Ed.). A brief history of the Committee on the occasion of its 25th anniversary. Chicago: University of Chicago, Committee on Human Development, 1965.

Cropley, A. J. Some psychological reflections on lifelong education. In R. H. Dave (Eds.), Foundations of life-long education. Oxford: Pergamon Press, 1976.

Danish, S. J. Human development and human services: A marriage proposal. In I. Iscoe, B. L. Bloom & C. B. Spielberger (Eds.), Community psychology in transition. New York: Halsted, 1977.

Datan, N., & Ginsberg, L. H. (Eds.). Life-span developmental psychology: Normative life crises. New York: Academic Press, 1975.

Datan, N., & Reese, H. W. (Eds.), Life-span developmental psychology: Dialectical perspectives on experimental research. New York: Academic Press, 1977.

Dave, R. H. (Ed.). Foundations of life-long education. Oxford: Pergamon Press, 1976.

Dave, R. H., & Lengrand, P. Lifelong education and learning. International Review of Education, 1974, 20, 425-537.

Dohrenwend, B. S., & Dohrenwend, P. B. (Eds.). Stressful life events. New York: Wiley, 1974.

Dubin, S. Obsolescence or lifelong education: A choice for the professional. American Psychologist, 1972, 486-498.

Dubin, S. The psychology of lifelong learning: New developments in the professions. International Review of Applied Psychology, 1974, 23, 17-31.

Elder, G. H. Age-differentiation in life course perspective. Annual Review of Sociology, 1975, 1, 165-190.

Gagne, R. M. Contributions of learning to human development. Psychological Review, 1968, 75, 177-191.

Gardner, E. G. & Monge, R. H. Adult age differences in cognitive abilities and educational background. Experimental Aging Research, 1977, 3, 337-383.

Gesell, A., Halverson, H. M., Thompson, H., & Ilg, F. The first five years of life: A guide to the study of the preschool child. New York: Harper & Row, 1940.

Gesell, A., & Ilg, F. Infant and child in the culture of today. New York: Harper & Row, 1943.

Goodnow, J. A test of milieu effects with some Piaget tasks. Psychological Monographs, 1962, 76, (36, Whole No. 555).

Goulet, L. R., & Baltes, P. B. (Eds.), Life-span developmental psychology: Research and theory. New York: Academic Press, 1970.

Granick, S., Kleban, M. H., & Weiss, A. D. Relationships between hearing loss and cognition in normally hearing aged persons. Journal of Gerontology, 1976, 31, 434-440.

Harris, D. B. Problems in formulating a scientific concept of development. D. B. Harris (Ed.), The concept of development. Minneapolis: University of Minnesota Press, 1957.

Havighurst, R. J. Developmental tasks and education. New York: McKay, 1972.

Hiemstra, R. Older adult learning. Educational Gerontologist, 1976, 1, 277-236.

Hine, W. D. The abilities of partially hearing children. British Journal of Educational Psychology, 1970, 40, 171-178.

Hollingworth, H. L. Mental growth and decline: A survey of

developmental psychology. New York: D. Appleton, 1927.

Horn, J. L. Personality and ability theory. In R. B. Cattell
(Ed.), Handbook of modern personality theory. New York:
Aldine, 1970.

Horn, J. L. Human ability systems. In P. B. Baltes (Ed.),
Life-span development and behavior (Vol. 1). New York:
Academic Press, 1978.

Horn, J. L., & Donaldson, G. On the myth of intellectual
decline in adulthood. American Psychologist, 1976, 31,
701-719.

Houle, C. O. The changing goals of education in the perspective of lifelong learning. International Review of
Education, 1974, 20, 430-445.

Hultsch, D. F., & Plemons, J. K. Life events and life-span
development. In P. B. Baltes & O. G. Brim, Jr. (Eds.),
Life-span development and behavior (Vol. 2). New York:
Academic Press, 1979, in press.

Huston-Stein, A., & Baltes, P. B. Theory and method in life-
span developmental psychology: Implications for child
development. In H. W. Reese (Ed.), Advances in child
development and behavior (Vol. 11). New York: Academic
Press, 1976.

Jarvik, L. Eisdorfer, C., & Blum, J. (Eds.). Intellectual
functioning in adults. New York: Springer, 1973.

Keniston, K. Psychological development and historical change.
Journal of Interdisciplinary History, 1971, 2, 330-345.

Kohn, M. L., & Schooler, C. The reciprocal effects of the
substantive complexity of work and intellectual flexibility: A longitudinal assessment. Unpublished manuscript, National Institute of Mental Health, Laboratory
of Socioenvironmental Studies, Washington, D. C., 1977.

Labouvie-Vief, G. Toward optimizing cognitive competence.
Educational Gerontology, 1976, 1, 75-92.

Labouvie-Vief, G. Adult cognitive development: In search of
alternative interpretations. Merrill Palmer Quarterly,
1978, in press.

Labouvie-Vief, C., & Chandler, M. J. Cognitive development
and life-span developmental theory: Idealistic versus

contextual perspectives. In P. B. Baltes (Ed.), Life-span development and behavior (Vol. 1). New York: Academic Press, 1978.

Lerner, R. M. Concepts and theories of human development. Reading, Mass.: Addison-Wesley, 1976.

Le Vine, R. A. Cross-cultural study in child psychology. In P. H. Mussen (Ed.), Carmichael's manual of child psychology (3rd ed.). New York: Wiley, 1970.

McCall, R. B. Challenges to a science of developmental psychology. Child Development, 1977, 48, 333-355.

Montada, L., & Filipp, S. Implications of life-span developmental psychology for childhood education. In H. W. Reese & L. P. Lipsitt (Eds.), Advances in child development. (Vol. 11). New York: Academic Press, 1976.

Nesselroade, J. R., & Baltes, P. B. Adolescent personality development and historical change: 1970-72. Monographs of the Society for Research in Child Development, 1974, 39, (Whole No. 154).

Nesselroade, J. R., & Reese, H. W. (Eds.). Life-span developmental psychology: Methodological issues. New York: Academic Press, 1973.

Neugarten, B. L. Continuities and discontinuities of psychological issues into adult life. Human Development, 1969, 12, 121-130.

Neugarten, B. L. , & Hagestad, G. Age and the life course. In R. Binstock & E. Shanas (Eds.), Handbook of aging and the social sciences. New York: Van Nostrand-Reinhold, 1976.

Neugarten, B. L., & Havighurst, R. J. (Eds). Social policy, social ethics, and the aging society. University of Chicago: Committee on Human Development, 1976.

Neugarten, B. L., & Havighurst, R. J. (Eds.). Extending the human life-span: Social policy and social ethics. Chicago: University of Chicago, Committee on Human Development, 1977.

Overton, W. F., & Reese, H. W. Models of development: Methodological implications. In J. R. Nesselroade & H. W. Reese (Eds.), Life-span developmental psychology: Methodological issues. New York: Academic Press, 1973.

Parelius, A. P. Lifelong education and age stratification.
American Behavioral Scientist, 1975, 19, 206-223.

Plemons, J. K., Willis, S. L., & Baltes, P. B. Modifiability
of fluid intelligence in aging: A short-term longitudinal training approach. Journal of Gerontology, 1978, 33,
224-231.

Porges, S. W. Cohort effects and apparent secular trends in
infant research. In K. F. Riegel & J. A. Meacham (Eds.),
The developing individual in a changing world (Vol. 2).
Chicago: Aldine, 1976.

Reese, H. W., & Overton, W. F. Models of development and
theories of development. In L. R. Goulet & P. B. Baltes
(Eds.), Life-span developmental psychology: Research and
theory. New York: Academic Press, 1970.

Reinert, G. Grundzüge einer Geschichte der Human-Entwick-
lungspsychologie. In H. Balmer (Ed.), Die Psychologie
des 20. Jahrhunderts (Vol 1). Zurich: Kindler, 1976.

Riegel, K. F. Dialectic operations: The final period of
cognitive development. Human Development, 1973, 16, 346-
370.

Riegel, K. F. The dialectics of time. In N. Datan & H. W.
Reese (Eds.), Life-span developmental psychology:
Dialectical perspectives on experimental research. New
York: Academic Press, 1977.

Riley, M. W. Age strata in social systems. In E. Shanas & R.
Binstock (Eds.), Handbook of aging and the social
sciences. New York: Reinhold-Van Nostrand, 1976.

Riley, M. W., Foner, A., Hess, B., & Toby, M. L. Social-
ization for the middle and later years. In D. Goslin
(Ed.), Handbook of socialization theory and research.
Chicago: McNally, 1969.

Riley, M. W. , Johnson, M., & Foner, A. (Eds.), Aging and
society (Vol. 3): A sociology of age stratification.
New York: Russell Sage, 1972.

Rosow, I. Socialization to old age. Berkeley, CA: University
of California Press, 1974.

Santrock, J. W. The relation of type and onset of father
absence to cognitive development. Child Development,
1972, 43, 455-469.

Schaie, K. W. A reinterpretation of age-related changes in cognitive structure and functioning. In L. R. Goulet & P. B. Baltes (Eds.), Life-span developmental psychology: Research and theory. New York: Academic Press, 1970.

Schaie, K. W. Towards a stage theory of adult cognitive development. Aging and Human Development, 1977-78, 8, 129-138.

Schaie K. W. The primary mental abilities in adulthood: An exploration in the development of psychometric intelligence. In P. B. Baltes & O. G. Brim, Jr. (Eds.), Life-span development and behavior (Vol. 2). New York: Academic Press, 1979, in press.

Schaie, K. W., & Baltes, P. B. Some faith helps to see the forest: A final comment on the Horn and Donaldson myth of the Baltes-Schaie position on adult intelligence. American Psychologist, 1977, 32, 1118-1120.

Schaie, K. W., & Parham, I. A. Cohort-sequential analyses of adult intellectual development. Developmental Psychology, 1977, 13, 649-653.

Schaie, K. W., & Quayhagen, M. Life-span educational psychology: Adulthood and old age. In J. Brandstaetter, G. Reinert, & K. A. Schneewind (Eds.), Probleme und Perspektiven der Paedagogischen Psychologie. Stuttgart: Klett, 1978.

Schaie, K. W., & Willis, S. L. Life-span development: Implications for education. Review of Educational Research, 1978, in press.

Sheldon, E. Parental child-rearing attitudes and their relationship to cognitive functioning of their pre-adolescent sons. Dissertation Abstracts, 1969, 29, (11-B), 4370.

Sigel, I. E. & Brodzinsky, D. M. Individual differences: A perspective for understanding intellectual development. In H. L. Hom & P. A. Robinsons (Eds.), Psychological processes in early education. New York: Academic Press, 1977.

Thomae, H. The concept of development and life-span developmental psychology. In P. B. Baltes & O. G. Brim, Jr. (Eds.), Life-span development and behavior (Vol. 2). New York: Academic Press, 1979, in press.

Toffler, A. Future shock. New York: Random House, 1970.

Wohlwill, J. F. Methodology and research strategy in the study of developmental change. In L. R. Goulet & P. B. Baltes (Eds.), Life-span developmental psychology: Research and theory. New York: Academic Press, 1970.

Wohlwill, J. R. The study of behavioral development. New York: Academic Press, 1973.

Wroczynski, R. Learning styles and lifelong education. International Review of Education, 1974, 20, 464-473.

Yeaxlee, A. B. Lifelong education: A sketch of the range and significance of the adult and education movement. London: Cassell, 1929.

Zajonc, R. B. Family configuration and intelligence. Science, 1976, 192, 227-236.

The Reciprocal Effects of the Substantive Complexity of Work and Intellectual Flexibility

A Longitudinal Assessment

Melvin L. Kohn and Carmi Schooler

From early Marx to "Work in America" it has been argued that work affects such facets of personality as values, orientation, and intellectual functioning. From early Taylor to the most recent personnel selection manuals it has been argued--or at any rate assumed--that personality is formed before occupational careers begin, with people fitting into and perhaps molding their jobs, but not being affected by their jobs. The issue of whether jobs affect or only reflect personality is obviously crucial to occupational social psychology. More than that, the issue of the nature and direction of causal effects in the relationship between occupational conditions and psychological functioning provides a critical test of a theoretical question central to the entire field of social structure and personality--whether social structure affects personality only through its influence on childhood socialization processes or also through a continuing influence during the entire life span.

In this paper we address the issue of the nature and direction of effects in the relationship between occupational conditions and psychological functioning by attempting to assess the reciprocal relationship between one pivotal dimension of occupational structure, the substantive complexity of work, and one pivotal dimension of psychological functioning, intellectual flexibility. We choose the substantive complexity of work as the occupational condition to be assessed in this analysis for

This is an abridged and revised version of a paper published in the American Journal of Sociology, July 1978.

three reasons: Our previous analyses have shown
substantive complexity to be a central element of
occupational structure--an important determinant of
occupational self-direction and an important "structural
imperative" of the job (Kohn and Schooler 1973, pp.
102-105). Moreover, substantive complexity is as strongly
correlated with psychological functioning as is any other
dimension of occupation we have examined (Kohn and
Schooler 1973, p. 104). Finally, we have excellent
descriptive information about the substantive complexity
of work, which we have been able to validate by comparison
to the objective job assessments of trained occupational
analysts (Kohn and Schooler 1973, p. 106).

Our choice of intellectual flexibility to be the
aspect of psychological functioning assessed in this
analysis is made in part because it offers us the greatest
challenge--intellectual flexibility obviously affects
recruitment into substantively complex jobs, and there is
every reason to expect it to be one of the most resistant
to change of all facets of psychological functioning we
have measured. Moreover, intellectual flexibility is so
important a part of psychological functioning that we must
not unthinkingly assume it to be entirely the product of
genetics and early life experience. Rather, we should
empirically test the possibility that intellectual
flexibility may be responsive to the experiences of adult
life.

In earlier analyses based on the data of a
cross-sectional survey carried out in 1964, we made
provisional assessments of the reciprocal relationship
between the substantive complexity of work and many facets
of psychological functioning, including intellectual
flexibility (Kohn and Schooler 1973; Kohn 1976). In those
analyses, we used a method called "two-stage least
squares", a relatively simple technique for estimating
reciprocal causal models. Our findings constitute prima
facie evidence that the substantive complexity of men's
work does affect their psychological functioning,
independently of the selection processes that draw men
into particular fields of work and independently of men's
efforts to mold their jobs to fit their needs, values, and
capacities. But cross-sectional data cannot provide
definitive evidence of causality; only analysis of
longitudinal data, measuring real change in real people,
can be definitive.

Moreover, while the cross-sectional data provided
retrospective information about the substantive complexity

of past jobs, it could not provide information about men's psychological functioning at the times they held those jobs. Thus, we had no way of statistically controlling earlier levels of intellectual flexibility in assessing the effect of substantive complexity (or anything else) on intellectual flexibility. And we could not examine lagged effects: for example, we could not assess the effects of earlier levels of intellectual flexibility on the substantive complexity of later jobs. Our analyses were necessarily limited to assessing the contemporaneous reciprocal effects, as of 1964, of the men's then-current levels of substantive complexity and psychological functioning.

Now we are able to assess the reciprocal effects of substantive complexity and intellectual flexibility much more adequately, for we have conducted a ten-year follow-up survey of a representative portion of our original sample. In this paper, we first describe and evaluate the data of the follow-up study. Then we explain the concepts, substantive complexity and intellectual flexibility, and develop "measurement models" for both of them. These models are designed to deal with the most perplexing problem of longitudinal analysis--that of separating errors in measurement from real change in the phenomena studied. Finally, we utilize the data provided by the measurement models to do a causal analysis of the reciprocal effects of substantive complexity and intellectual flexibility.

The Longitudinal Data

The earlier, cross-sectional analyses were based on interviews conducted in 1964 with a sample of 3101 men, representative of all men employed in civilian occupations in the United States. (For more specific information on sample and research design, see Kohn 1969, pp. 235-64.)

In 1974 the National Opinion Research Center (N.O.R.C.) carried out a follow-up survey for us, interviewing a representative sample of approximately one-fourth of those men who were less than 65 years old. The age limitation was imposed to increase the probability that the men in the follow-up study would still be in the labor force.

In this as in all longitudinal studies, the question of the representativeness of the follow-up sample is

crucial for assessing the accuracy of any analyses we do.[1]
Of the 883 men whom we randomly selected for the follow-up
study, N.O.R.C. succeeded in locating 820 (i.e., 93%) ten
years after the original survey—in itself an interesting
social fact.   Apparently men who live their lives in the
ordinary institutions of the society, although they may
change residences a very great deal, can be traced, given
a modicum of cooperation from the post office, the
telephone company, past employers, and unions.

Of the 820 men located, 35 had died.   Of the
remaining 785 men, N.O.R.C. actually re-interviewed 687,
i.e., 78% of those originally selected and 88% of those
located and found to be alive.   In terms of current
experience in survey research, these are certainly
acceptable figures.   But we must nevertheless ask: Are
the men who were re-interviewed representative of all
those men whom we meant to interview?   Can we generalize
safely to the larger universe?   We attempt to answer these
questions by two types of analysis.

The first type of analysis involves systematic
comparison of the social and psychological characteristics
of the men who were re-interviewed with those of a truly
representative sample of the under-65 population.   We are
in an optimum position to do this, for the men who were
randomly excepted from the follow-up study constitute a
representative subsample of the overall sample and thus
are an appropriate comparison group.   The differences
between the two subsamples are few and small in magnitude:
the men who were re-interviewed were, as of the time of
the original interviews, a little more intellectually
flexible, somewhat more trustful, slightly lower in
self-confidence, and somewhat more "liberal" in their
religious backgrounds than were those in the comparison
group.   But the two groups do not differ significantly in
most of the characteristics important to our
analyses—e.g., education, social class, major
occupational characteristics, age, and even urbanicity.

Our second method of assessing the
representativeness of the follow-up sample is to repeat
the major substantive analyses, again using the 1964 data,
but this time limiting the analyses to those men whom we
succeeded in re-interviewing in 1974.   The rationale is
that insofar as we get the same results from analyses of
the follow-up subsample as those we got from the total

---

[1]/For an assessment of the representativeness of the
original sample, see Kohn 1969:   Appendix C.

sample, we can be confident that the subsample provides a good base from which to generalize to the larger population. We have repeated all the principal analyses of the relationships among social class, occupational conditions, and psychological functioning. The smaller size of the subsample means that several secondary avenues cannot be explored and that some findings are no longer statistically significant. But the main findings hold up uniformly well. Thus, we can proceed to analyze the longitudinal data with confidence that whatever we find can be generalized to the larger population of employed men in the United States.

Unreliability and Change

We now face the core technical problem in longitudinal analysis--how to separate unreliability of measurement from real change in the phenomena studied. In principle, unreliability in the measurement of the independent variables is especially likely to confound causal analysis. In our case, both substantive complexity and intellectual flexibility serve as principal independent variables vis-a-vis each other; it is the relative magnitude of their effects that is centrally at issue. Therefore, we need to assess how much of any apparent change in substantive complexity represents real change in men's job conditions over the 10-year interval between the two surveys, and how much is a function of unreliability in the measuring instruments. Similarly, we need to assess how much of any apparent change in intellectual flexibility represents real change in the men's cognitive functioning and how much is a result of measurement error.

Recently, Joreskog and his associates have introduced powerful new procedures for using maximum-likelihood confirmatory factor analysis to separate unreliability from change. (See Joreskog 1969, 1973; Joreskog and Sorbom, 1976.) The essence of these methods is the use of multiple indicators for each principal concept, inferring from the covariation of the indicators the degree to which each reflects the underlying concept that they all are hypothesized to reflect and the degree to which each reflects anything else, which for measurement purposes is considered to be error. The test of our success in differentiating "true scores" on the underlying concept from errors in the indicators is how well the hypothesized model reproduces the original variance-covariance matrix of the indicators.

The first step in the use of these procedures is to develop "measurement models" for the principal concepts--models that will later form the basis for a causal analysis. The measurement models must specify the relationships of indicators to concepts, take account of unreliability (or "measurement error") in all the items that measure a concept, and allow for the possibility that measurement errors are correlated in repeated measurements of the same phenomena. For example, any errors in the information obtained in 1964 about the complexity of men's work with "things," or in our coding of this information, might well be correlated with errors in the same type of information in 1974. Such correlated error in any constituent item might make our index of substantive complexity seem more stable or less stable than it really is. Before assessing changes, and the reasons for such changes, in the substantive complexity of work, we must remove the effects of correlated errors in measurement of the indicators of this concept.

A Measurement Model

For Substantive Complexity

By the substantive complexity of work we mean the degree to which the work, in its very substance, requires thought and independent judgment. Substantively complex work, by its very nature, requires making many decisions that must take into account ill-defined or apparently conflicting contingencies. Although, in general, work with data or with people is likely to be more complex than work with things, this is not always the case, and an index of the overall complexity of the work should reflect its degree of complexity in each of these three types of activity. Work with things can vary in complexity from ditch-digging to sculpting; similarly, work with people can vary in complexity from receiving simple directions or orders to giving legal advice; and work with data can vary from reading instructions to synthesizing abstract conceptual systems.

Our information about the substantive complexity of men's work is derived from detailed questioning of each respondent about his work with things, with data or ideas, and with people. The men's answers to these detailed questions provided the basis for seven ratings: appraisals of the complexity of each man's work with things, with data, and with people; an appraisal of the overall complexity of his work, regardless of whether he works primarily with data, with people, or with things;

and estimates of the amount of time he spends working at
each type of activity. In earlier analyses, we subjected
these seven ratings to a one-dimensional exploratory
factor analysis, which we then used as the basis for
creating factor scores.

Now, instead of using exploratory factor analysis to
create a single composite score, we treat all seven
ratings of the 1964 job as "indicators" of the underlying
but not directly measured concept, the substantive
complexity of that job. Each indicator is conceived to
reflect the underlying concept, which it measures only
imperfectly, together with some degree of "error" in
measurement. (See Alwin 1973, p. 259 and note 2.) The
follow-up survey asks the same questions and makes the
same seven ratings. Again, we treat these ratings as
indicators of the underlying concept, in this instance the
substantive complexity of the job held at the time of the
1974 interview. Again, we conceive of each indicator as
reflecting the underlying concept, together with some
degree of measurement error. We also allow for the
possibility that errors of measurement are correlated over
time—that whatever errors there may be in the measurement
of complexity of work with things in the 1964 job, for
example, may be correlated with errors in the measurement
of complexity of work with things in the 1974 job.

We have information also about the complexity of
each man's work in two of his earlier jobs, the first job
he held for six months or longer, and the job he held
immediately before his 1964 job. Both of these measures
are approximate scores, based on extrapolations from
limited job history information (see Kohn and Schooler
1973, pp. 111-12 and note 21). In our earlier analyses,
we treated these as two separate variables. In the
present analysis, we have no real need for measures of
substantive complexity at two separate times before 1964.
But the logic of our measurement model calls for using
multiple indicators of important concepts whenever it is
possible to do so; it is the multiplicity of indicators
that enables us to differentiate unreliability of
measurement from change in true scores. We therefore
treat these two measures as indicators of a single
concept, "earlier" substantive complexity.

The overall "fit" of this model to the data, based
on a chi-squared goodness of fit test, is fairly good:
the total chi-square is 563.56, with 94 degrees of
freedom, for a ratio of 5.60 per degree of freedom. (In
this test, chi-square is a function of the discrepancies

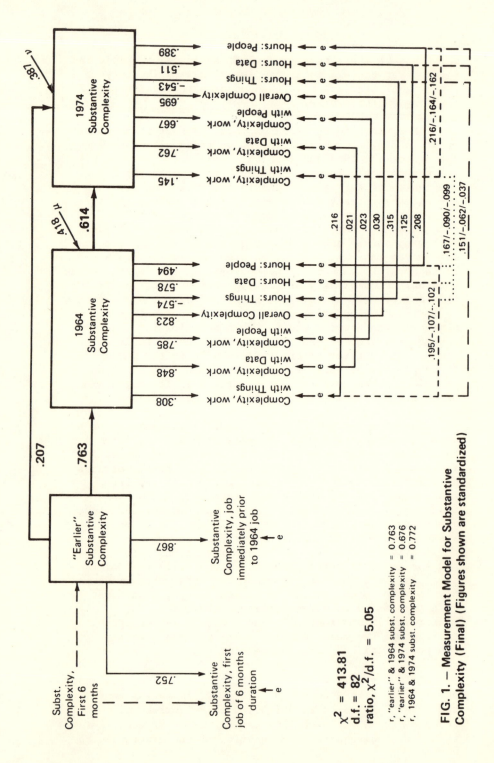

FIG. 1. — Measurement Model for Substantive Complexity (Final) (Figures shown are standardized)

$x^2 = 413.81$
d.f. = 82
ratio, x^2/d.f. = 5.05

r, "earlier" & 1964 subst. complexity = 0.763
r, "earlier" & 1974 subst. complexity = 0.676
r, 1964 & 1974 subst. complexity   = 0.772

between the actual variance-covariance matrix and the
variance-covariance matrix implied by the measurement
model. Therefore, the better the fit, the smaller the
chi-square per degree of freedom.) But an examination of
the first-order partial derivatives of the
maximum-likelihood function (see Sorbom 1975) indicates
that the fit of model to data can be improved by taking
into account other correlated errors of
measurement—notably, between the complexity of work with
things and the amount of time spent working with things,
with data, and with people, both intra-time and over time.
With these errors allowed to correlate (see Figure 1), the
overall chi-square is 413.81, with 82 degrees of freedom,
for a ratio of 5.05, which is quite good for so complex a
model, based on so large a sample.[1] All the parameters of
this model are consistent with our theoretical intent. In
particular, the complexity of work with data and with
people and the overall complexity of the work are shown to
bear a strong positive relationship to the underlying
concept, while the amount of time spent working with
things is shown to be strongly negatively related to the
concept, in both 1964 and 1974.

The most interesting information provided by the
measurement model depicted in Figure 1 is the estimate of
the overall stability in job complexity. The stability,
as expected, is substantial; for example, the path from
the substantive complexity of the 1964 job to that of the
1974 job is 0.61 and the correlation between the two is
0.77. The actual "effect" of earlier jobs on later jobs,
as compared to the "effect" of other variables, can only
be assessed in the causal analyses to come, when other
independent variables are simultaneously considered. What
the measurement model does tell us is that there has been
considerable stability in the substantive complexity of
the men's jobs over the course of their careers.

A Measurement Model

For Intellectual Flexibility

Our index of intellectual flexibility is meant to
reflect men's actual intellectual performance in the

---

[1] In Figure 1, in all subsequent Figures, and in the
text, we present standardized values. These are more
easily comprehended than are metric values and using
standardized values makes it possible to compare
indicators in the measurement models and causal paths in
the structural equation models. But all computations have
been based on unstandardized variance-covariance matrices.

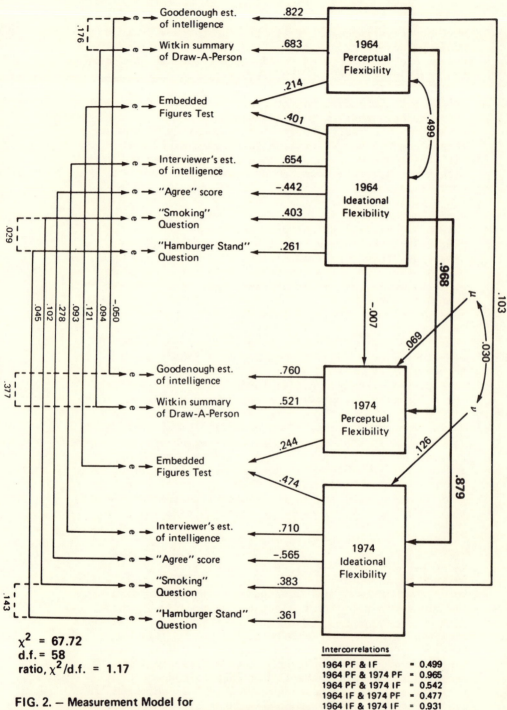

FIG. 2. — Measurement Model for
Intellectual Flexibility (Figures shown are standardized)

χ^2 = 67.72
d.f. = 58
ratio, χ^2/d.f. = 1.17

Intercorrelations

1964 PF & IF	= 0.499
1964 PF & 1974 PF	= 0.965
1964 PF & 1974 IF	= 0.542
1964 IF & 1974 PF	= 0.477
1964 IF & 1974 IF	= 0.931
1974 PF & 1974 IF	= 0.549

interview situation. In the 1964 interview, we sampled a
variety of indicators--including the men's answers to
seemingly simple but highly revealing cognitive problems
involving well-known issues, their handling of perceptual
and projective tests, their propensity to "agree" when
asked agree-disagree questions, and the impression they
made on the interviewer during a long session that
required a great deal of thought and reflection. None of
these indicators is assumed to be completely valid; but we
do assume that all the indicators reflect, in some
substantial degree, men's flexibility in attempting to
cope with the intellectual demands of a complex situation.

We claim neither that this index measures "innate"
intellectual ability, nor that intellectual flexibility
evidenced in the interview situation is necessarily
identical to intellectual flexibility as it might be
manifested in other situations; we do not have enough
information about the situational variability of
intellectual functioning to be certain. We do claim that
our index reflects men's actual intellectual functioning
in a non-work situation that seemed to elicit considerable
intellectual effort from nearly all the respondents. That
our index is not artifactual, and that it measures an
enduring characteristic, is attested to by the
evidence--to be presented shortly--of its remarkably high
stability over time. Spaeth's (1976) analysis adds to the
credibility of the index by showing that the correlations
between an earlier variant of our index and various social
phenomena are similar to those for more conventional
indices of intellectual functioning.

More concretely and specifically, our index (see
Figure 2) is based on seven indicators of each man's
intellectual performance. These are: (1) The Goodenough
estimate of his intelligence (see Witkin, et al. 1962),
based on a detailed evaluation of the Draw-A-Person test.
(2) Witkin's (1962) appraisal of the sophistication of
body-concept in the Draw-A-Person test. (3) A summary
score for his performance on a portion of the Embedded
Figures test (see Witkin, et al. 1962). (4) The
interviewer's appraisal of the man's intelligence. (5)
The frequency with which he agreed when asked the many
agree-disagree questions included in the interview. (6) A
rating of the adequacy of his answer to the apparently
simple cognitive problem: "What are all the arguments you
can think of for and against allowing cigarette
commercials on TV?" (7) A rating of the adequacy of his

answer to another relatively simple cognitive problem, "Suppose you wanted to open a hamburger stand and there were two locations available. What questions would you consider in deciding which of the two locations offers a better business opportunity?"

In the earlier analyses of the 1964 data, we performed an orthogonal principal components factor analysis of these various manifestations of intellectual flexibility. This analysis yielded two dimensions, one primarily perceptual, the other ideational. Since the ideational component of intellectual flexibility is of much greater theoretical interest, our analyses have focused on that dimension.

In the follow-up study, we secured entirely comparable data, after elaborate pre-testing to be certain that the cognitive problems had the same meaning in 1974 as in 1964. The measurement model we now employ for intellectual flexibility is similar to that for substantive complexity in most respects, with the following exceptions. First, following the logic of the two-factor model derived from the earlier exploratory factor analysis, we posit two concepts underlying the seven indicators. Second, we have no assessments of intellectual flexibility prior to 1964, so there is nothing comparable to "earlier" substantive complexity. Third, to take into account that two of our indicators are based on the same task, the Draw-a-Person test, we allow their errors to be correlated. Finally, following a lead provided by the first-order partial derivatives, we also allow for the possibility of correlated error between the two cognitive problems.

We get slightly different estimates of the parameters of the measurement model, depending on whether we posit (as in the earlier analysis) that the two underlying concepts are necessarily orthogonal to each other or that they are possibly correlated with one another. The nonorthogonal model provides a significantly better fit to the data, so we shall employ it in the causal analyses that follow. (In any event, estimates of the reciprocal effects of substantive complexity and ideational flexibility prove to be virtually identical whether based on orthogonal or on nonorthogonal measurement models of intellectual flexibility.)

Figure 2 depicts the measurement model for intellectual flexibility, with the two underlying concepts allowed to correlate. The model shows that some of the indicators of intellectual flexibility are not especially reliable; this is the very reason we thought it necessary to construct a measurement model that would differentiate unreliability of measurement from actual intellectual functioning. Judging by the goodness-of-fit test, the model is successful in achieving this objective: the overall chi-square is 67.72, with 58 degrees of freedom, for a ratio of 1.17, which means that the model provides a very good approximation to the actual variances and covariances of the indicators.

From this model, we learn that the path from men's levels of ideational flexibility in 1964 to their levels of ideational flexibility in 1974, shorn of measurement error, is a very substantial 0.88 and that the correlation betwen the two is an even higher 0.93. We conclude that there has been great stability in men's levels of ideational flexibility over the 10-year period.[1] The question for causal analysis is whether, despite this overall stability, there has been enough individual change for job conditions to have had much of an effect.

Causal Analysis: The Reciprocal Effects

of Substantive Complexity and

Intellectual Flexibility

To do structural equation causal analyses, we have computed the variances and the (unstandardized) covariances between the "true scores" for job complexity at the various stages of career, intellectual flexibility in 1964 and in 1974, and all the other variables that will enter into the analyses.[2] These variances and

---

[1] Parenthetically, the correlation between an index of ideational flexibility based on factor scores derived from exploratory factor analysis of the 1964 data and a similar index based on the same factor loadings for 1974 is a much lower 0.59. This finding dramatically illustrates the moral that methodologists have long been preaching -- that correlations may be radically understated when they are not corrected for the attenuation that results from unreliability of measurement.

[2] Our procedure has been to develop measurement models independently for each concept, compute the covariances among "true scores", and use these covariances as the data for causal analysis. Computing the covariances of the concepts can be done with either the ACOVS or LISREL

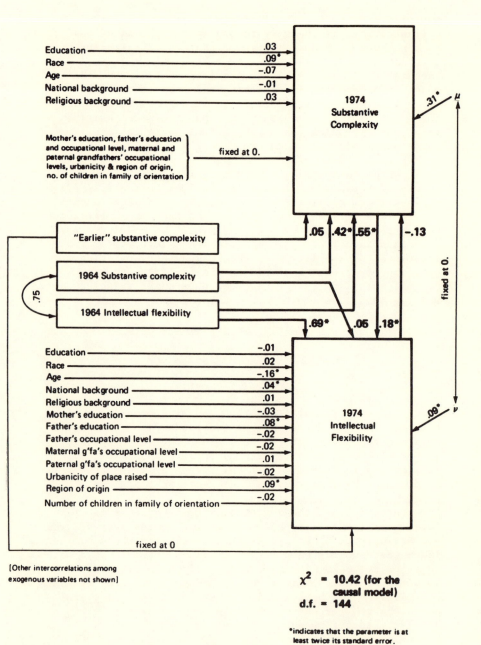

FIG. 3. – The Reciprocal Effects of Substantive Complexity and Intellectual Flexibility:
Full Model (Figures shown are standardized)

covariances are the data on which the causal models of the reciprocal relationship between substantive complexity and intellectual flexibility are based. [1]

A reciprocal relationship can occur contemporaneously (albeit not necessarily instantaneously) or more gradually over time. Our earlier analyses, using cross-sectional data, could consider only contemporaneous effects. But there is no reason in principle why substantive complexity and intellectual flexibility might not affect each other both contemporaneously and more gradually over time. We shall therefore assess causal models that allow the possibility of both contemporaneous and "lagged" reciprocal effects (see Figure 3). Since our concern in these analyses is entirely with the ideational component of intellectual flexibility, we shall henceforth use the terms ideational flexibility and intellectual flexibility interchangeably and limit the analyses to ideational flexibility. [2]

The model depicted in Figure 3 includes as potentially pertinent exogenous variables all social characteristics that prior research literature and our own earlier analyses give us any reason to believe might

computer programs. Using either procedure, one develops models that combine the principal features of two or more measurement models. In developing these combined models, the crucial requirement is to fix, at the values derived from the measurement models, those parameters that define the relationships between concepts and their indicators (e.g., the paths from concepts to indicators, the residuals for the indicators, and the correlations among those residuals) while not inadvertently constraining the interrelationships of the concepts (e.g., when using LISREL, by fixing causal paths at zero or at some other value instead of allowing them to be free, or by fixing the unexplained variance of any of the concepts).

[1] In developing the causal (i.e., linear structural equation) models, we employed the LISREL computer program (Joreskog and van Thillo 1972), as subsequently modified by Ronald Schoenberg.

[2] In fact, the effect of substantive complexity on perceptual flexibility is of approximately the same magnitude as its effect on ideational flexibility. But we cannot assess the reciprocal effect, of perceptual flexibility on substantive complexity, because the 1964 and 1974 measures of perceptual flexibility are so highly

affect either substantive complexity or intellectual
flexibility. We thus include in the model the
respondent's own age and level of education, his mother's
and his father's levels of education, his father's
occupational level, his maternal and paternal
grandfathers' occupational levels, his race, national
background, and religious background, the urbanicity and
region of the country of the principal place where he was
raised, and even the number of brothers and sisters he
had. 1/ We also include as exogenous variables the
respondent's 1964 levels of substantive complexity and
intellectual flexibility, as well as the substantive
complexity of his "earlier" (pre-1964) jobs.

For the model to be adequately identified, the
direct effects of one or more exogenous variables on 1974
intellectual flexibility must be assumed to be zero;
similarly, the direct effects of one or more exogenous
variables on 1974 substantive complexity must also be
assumed to be zero; otherwise there will be too little
empirical information to solve the equations
unequivocally.2/ Therefore, we posit that background

---

correlated (at 0.96) that we encounter insuperable
problems of multicollinearity.

1/ The indices of national background, region, and
religious background are linear approximations to these
nonlinear concepts. In our present use, these linearized
indices represent slight underestimates of what would be
shown in a more complicated dummy variable analysis. The
rationale for these linearizations is given in Schooler
1972, 1976. Essentially, all three indices are ordered in
terms of environmental complexity: national background,
on the basis of how long it has been since the social
organization of the nation's agriculture passed beyond
feudalism; region of the United States, on the basis of
industrialization and expenditures for education; and
religion, on the basis of fundamentalism.

2/ In contemporaneous effects models (and other
"nonrecursive" models), the number of parameters to be
estimated will be greater than the amount of information
provided by the intercorrelations among the variables,
unless some assumptions are imposed on the model, usually
by setting some path(s) to zero. (Alternatively, one can
impose other restrictions on the model, e.g., as we have
in fact done, by not allowing the residuals to be
correlated.) The problem of insufficient information is
generally referred to as the "identification" problem and

characteristics that would not be interpreted as job
credentials by employers (even by discriminatory
employers) do not directly affect the substantive
complexity of the 1974 job; these variables are thus used
as "instruments" to identify the equation. The rationale
is that these variables--maternal and paternal education,
paternal occupational level, maternal and paternal
grandfathers' occupational levels, urbanicity and region
of origin, and number of children in the parental
family--may very likely have affected men's job placement
earlier in their careers. By the time that men are at
least ten years into their careers, though, these
variables should no longer have any direct effect on the
substantive complexity of their jobs, certainly not when
the substantive complexity of their "earlier" and 1964
jobs are statistically controlled. Similarly, we posit
that the substantive complexity of "earlier" jobs should
have no direct effect on the men's intellectual
flexibility in 1974, when the substantive complexity of
their 1964 and 1974 jobs are statistically controlled.

As Figure 3 shows, a very important determinant of
the substantive complexity of the jobs the men held in
1974 is, of course, the substantive complexity of the jobs
they held ten years before; an even more important
determinant of their intellectual flexibility in 1974 is
their intellectual flexibility at the earlier time. As we
learned from the measurement models, both phenomena,
particularly intellectual flexibility, are stable.
Nevertheless, the reciprocal effects of substantive
complexity and intellectual flexibility are considerable.

The effect of substantive complexity on
intellectual flexibility is approximately one-fourth as
great as the effect of men's 10-year earlier levels of
intellectual flexibility. This effect is essentially
contemporaneous:[1] The lagged path from 1964 substantive

---

a variable that is used to help solve the identification
problem is called an "instrument." For lucid discussions
of this complex topic, see Duncan 1975, pp. 81-90; and
Heise 1975, pp. 160-81.

[1]/A cautionary note is in order here. Our analysis
does not take into account the length of time the men have
been in their present jobs; thus, all we mean by
"contemporaneous" is that the effect results from the job
currently held (however long it has been held, short of
ten years), not from any previous job. A more exact

complexity to 1974 intellectual flexibility is a
statistically nonsignificant 0.05, while the
contemporaneous path from 1974 substantive complexity is a
more substantial and statistically significant 0.18.

A path of 0.18 might not in ordinary circumstances
be considered especially striking; but a continuing effect
of this magnitude on so stable a phenomenon as
intellectual flexibility is impressive, for the cumulative
impact is much greater than the immediate effect at any
one time. Continuing effects, even small-to-moderate
continuing effects, on highly stable phenomena become
magnified in importance. The effect of the substantive
complexity of work on intellectual flexibility is
especially noteworthy when we take into account that we
are dealing with men no younger than 26 years of age, who
are at least ten years into their occupational careers.

The reciprocal effect of intellectual flexibility
on substantive complexity is even more
impressive—surpassing that of the substantive complexity
of the 1964 job. This effect is entirely lagged, i.e., it
is the men's intellectual flexibility in 1964, not
contemporaneously, that significantly affects the
substantive complexity of their 1974 jobs. The
longitudinal analysis thus demonstrates something that no
cross-sectional analysis could show—that, over time, the
relationship between substantive complexity and
intellectual flexibility is truly reciprocal. The effect
of substantive complexity on intellectual flexibility is
more rapid: current job demands affect current thinking
processes. Intellectual flexibility, by contrast, has a
delayed effect on substantive complexity: current
intellectual flexibility has scant effect on current job
demands, but it will have a sizeable effect on the further
course of one's career. The cross-sectional analysis
portrayed only part of this process, making it seem as if
the relationship between the substantive complexity of
work and psychological functioning were mainly
unidirectional, with work affecting psychological
functioning but not the reverse. The longitudinal
analysis portrays a more intricate and more interesting,
truly reciprocal, process.

Have we somehow misspecified the equations, leaving

---

appraisal of the timing of job effects would be
exceedingly difficult to accomplish without measurements
of both substantive complexity and intellectual
flexibility at more frequent intervals than we have made.

out some important variables that might alter the overall
picture or in some other way misconceiving the true
picture? Since no structural model can ever be "proved"
(Duncan 1975), but can only be compared to other plausible
models, all reasonable alternatives must be considered.

One indication that the equations have not been
seriously misspecified is that if we allow the residuals
for 1974 substantive complexity and 1974 intellectual
flexibility to be correlated, the correlation proves to be
nonsignificant and the estimates of all parameters remain
essentially unchanged. Thus, it seems unlikely that some
important variable affecting both substantive complexity
and intellectual flexibility has been left out of the
model. Moreover, the results do not depend on our choice
of instruments, for using a variety of other instruments
does not appreciably change the results. Nor do our
findings result from the presence of statistically
nonsignificant background variables in the model, for
deleting the nonsignificant background variables from the
predictive equations does not affect our conclusions. In
particular, the effect of substantive complexity on
intellectual flexibility is slightly strengthened by the
deletion of background variables that do not have
statistically significant effects. The model is robust,
whatever reasonable modifications we try.

Finally, our findings do not result from our having
fixed the values of the measurement models before
estimating the causal model (see Burt 1973). We have
confirmed the causal model by developing a "full-
information model," in which both measurement and causal
parameters are estimated simultaneously. This model
confirms both the measurement models and the causal model
depicted in Figure 3. In particular, it shows the effect
of substantive complexity on intellectual flexibility to
be contemporaneous and of the same magnitude as previously
shown. The effect of intellectual flexibility on
substantive complexity is again shown to be lagged. The
magnitude of this path, too, is exactly the same as in
Figure 3.

The one anomaly in the model shown in Figure 3 and
in the corresponding full-information model is that the
path from 1974 intellectual flexibility to 1974
substantive complexity is not just statistically
nonsignificant, it is negative. Despite its statistical
nonsignificance, the existence of such a negative path
suggests a problem of multicollinearity, probably
resulting from the very high correlation (r=0.93) between

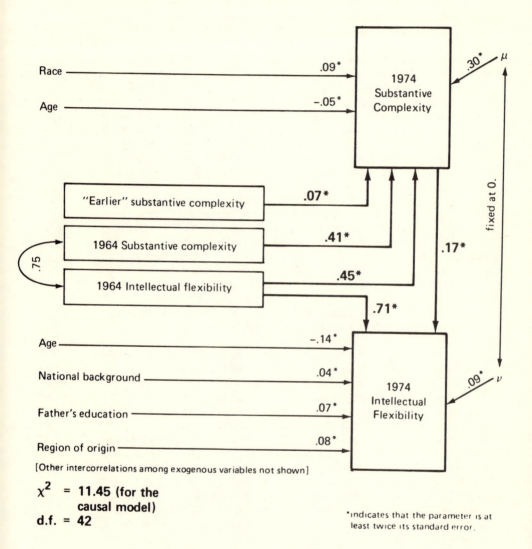

FIG. 4. — The Reciprocal Effects of Substantive Complexity
and Intellectual Flexibility: Significant Paths Only
(Figures shown are standardized)

1964 and 1974 intellectual flexibility. When we use
indices of both 1964 and 1974 intellectual flexibility as
independent variables vis-a-vis substantive complexity, we
probably exaggerate the importance of 1964 intellectual
flexibility while creating an artificially negative effect
for 1974 intellectual flexibility. A proper assessment of
the effect of intellectual flexibility on substantive
complexity requires our dropping the statistically
nonsignificant contemporaneous path from the model.
Similarly, a proper assessment of the effect of
substantive complexity on intellectual flexibility
requires our dropping the statistically nonsignificant
lagged path from the model. Therefore, in Figure 4 we
delete these (and all other) nonsignificant paths and
re-estimate the model. This, we believe, represents the
most accurate assessment that can be made of the overall
effects of substantive complexity and intellectual
flexibility on each other.

     This model shows the contemporaneous effect of
substantive complexity on intellectual flexibility to be
of virtually the same magnitude (a path of 0.17) as that
shown in Figure 3. Even with a slightly higher estimate
of the stability of intellectual flexibility (at 0.71),
the effect of substantive complexity on intellectual
flexibility remains nearly one-fourth as great as that of
the men's 10-year earlier levels of intellectual
flexibility.

     The lagged effect of intellectual flexibility on
substantive complexity (a path of 0.45) is not quite so
great as it had appeared to be before we removed the
nonsignificant, negative contemporaneous path in Figure 4,
but by any other standard it is very large. Intellectual
flexibility surpasses even the substantive complexity of
men's 1964 jobs as a determinant of the substantive
complexity of their 1974 jobs.

     Just as we did for the model depicted in Figure 3,
we have confirmed Figure 4 by developing a "full
information model," in which measurement and causal
parameters are simultaneously estimated.[1] All parameters
of the measurement models for both substantive complexity
and intellectual flexibility are very close to those shown

_____
[1]The chi-square for the full-information model
comparable to Figure 3 is 1035.23, with 546 degrees of
freedom, for a ratio of 1.90, a remarkably good fit of
model to data for so complex a model based on so large a
number of cases. The chi-square for the full-information

in Figures 1 and 2, most of them nearly identical, none differing by more than 0.03. The causal model, too, is confirmed, the contemporaneous path from substantive complexity to intellectual flexibility being exactly as we had found it to be in Figure 4 (0.17), the lagged path from intellectual flexibility to substantive complexity being slightly lower (0.41 instead of 0.45). All other causal parameters are very close to those shown in Figure 4.

The data thus demonstrate, beyond reasonable doubt, what heretofore could be stated as only a plausible thesis buttressed by presumptive evidence--that the substantive complexity of men's work both considerably affects, and is considerably affected by, their intellectual flexibility. [1]

model comparable to Figure 4 is nearly the same--1036.68, with 548 degrees of freedom, for a ratio of 1.89. Nothing is lost in the fit of model to data in simplifying the model.

[1] Although our primary interest is the reciprocal effects of substantive complexity and intellectual flexibility, the model is also instructive in telling us about the effects of social background on men's jobs and cognitive functioning in mid- and later-career. By the time men are at least ten years into their occupational careers, only race and age continue to have direct effects on the substantive complexity of their jobs; other aspects of social background have certainly affected the substantive complexity of earlier jobs, but by this stage of career not even education has a statistically significant direct effect. Age is negatively related to 1974 substantive complexity, when the substantive complexity of prior jobs is statistically controlled. Since the correlation in 1964 was positive, this probably indicates that over the ten-year period, the younger men in the sample have been closing the gap. It is possible, though, that our finding reflects a curvilinear relationship between age and substantive complexity or a cohort effect. Similarly, the data suggest that blacks are catching up with whites in the substantive complexity of their jobs, probably a reflection of lessening discrimination. In their effects on intellectual flexibility, age, national background, father's education, and region of origin (not education, race, size of parental family, or urbanicity) continue to be statistically significant, when prior intellectual

Discussion

There are several limitations to the analyses reported in this paper: some, we hope to remedy in further analyses; the others may be beyond our ingenuity or the scope of our data.

One obvious limitation is that our analysis has thus far been restricted to substantive complexity and intellectual flexibility. In our further work, we intend to develop measurement models for other facets of occupational structure and for other facets of psychological functioning. Our hope is to develop ultimately a causal model of the overall relationship between occupational structure and psychological functioning.

Second, the present analysis, as was true of all our previous analyses of occupational conditions, deals only with men. We are now analyzing data for women, and in the near future intend to report on the relationship between women's occupational conditions and their psychological functioning.

A third limitation is that, although our measurement models take account of unreliability in indicators of the two central concepts, they have not dealt with possible unreliability of measurement for education, race, age, or any other aspect of social background. Our own data do not provide any solid basis for assessing reliability of measurement of these variables, and we are dubious about using reliability coefficients derived from other bodies of data as the basis for correcting correlations for attenuation. It would probably not make any real difference in the causal analysis. But, without evidence, the issue must be left unresolved.

Fourth, conspicuously lacking in our treatment of these data is a systematic analysis of "career" patterns. We have treated prior jobs (and even the same job, held ten years earlier) as if all series of jobs were equally continuous or discontinuous along some meaningful career line. But a more realistic conceptualization would have to take account that some job changes represent logical progression in a meaningful sequence, while others

flexibility is statistically controlled. None of these variables, not even age, has as large an effect on intellectual flexibility as does the substantive complexity of work.

represent shifts out of one career sequence, perhaps into another. We know of no really satisfactory way of dealing with this issue.

Fifth, both our measurement models and our causal models assume that relationships among variables are essentially the same for all segments of the work force. The assumption is obviously testable, and we hope to test it, although we recognize that a thorough assessment may require a much larger body of data than ours. It would be especially desirable to examine these models separately for workers at different ages and at different stages of career.

Sixth, as must be apparent to the reader, changes in occupational circumstances are not the only changes that people experience in a ten-year interval: some marry, or divorce, or become widowed; traumas and joyous events occur; these and other occurrences may exacerbate, mitigate, or deflect the processes our models depict. We have information about these events, but it is too early in the analytic process to tell whether the depth of the data and the size of the sample are adequate for analyzing the part they play in the ongoing process.

Despite these limitations, we believe that we have shown, more definitively than has ever been shown before, that the relationship between occupational conditions and psychological functioning is reciprocal: people's occupational conditions both affect and are affected by their psychological functioning.

These findings come down solidly in support of those who see occupational conditions as affecting personality and in opposition to those who see the relationship between occupational conditions and personality as resulting solely from selective recruitment and job-molding. We do not deny that personality has great importance in determining who go into what types of jobs and how they perform those jobs; in fact, our analyses underline the importance of these processes. But that has never been seriously at issue. What has been disputed is whether the reverse phenomenon—of job conditions molding personality—also occurs. The evidence of our study unequivocally supports the position that it does occur. Thus our findings bear directly on an issue central to the field of social structure and personality— whether social-structural conditions affect personality only during childhood socialization or continue to affect personality throughout adulthood. Here is clear evidence

that one important facet of social structure--the
substantive complexity of work--directly affects adult
personality.

In particular, this study adds to and helps specify
the growing evidence that the structure of the environment
has an important effect on cognitive development (see
Rosenbaum 1976) and that cognitive processes do not become
impervious to environmental influence after adolescence or
early adulthood, but continue to show "plasticity"
throughout the life span (see Baltes 1968.) Our findings
reinforce this conclusion by showing that intellectual
flexibility continues to be responsive to experience well
into mid-career and probably beyond. In fact, it appears
that the remarkable stability of intellectual flexibility
reflects, at least in part, stability in people's life
circumstances. Intellectual flexibility is
ever-responsive to changes in the substantive complexity
of people's work; for most people, though, the substantive
complexity of work does not fluctuate markedly.

The reciprocal relationship between substantive
complexity and intellectual flexibility implies an
internal dynamic by which relatively small differences in
substantive complexity at early stages of career may
become magnified into larger differences in both
substantive complexity and intellectual flexibility later
in the career. If two men of equivalent intellectual
flexibility were to start their careers in jobs differing
in substantive complexity, the man in the more complex job
would be likely to outstrip the other in further
intellectual growth. This, in time, might lead to his
attaining jobs of greater complexity, further affecting
his intellectual growth. Meantime, the man in the less
complex job would develop intellectually at a slower pace,
perhaps not at all, and in the extreme case might even
decline in his intellectual functioning. As a result,
small differences in the substantive complexity of early
jobs might lead to increasing differences in intellectual
development.

This study demonstrates as well the importance of
the impact of intellectual flexibility on substantive
complexity. We think it noteworthy that this effect
appears to be lagged, rather than contemporaneous. The
implication is that the structure of most jobs does not
permit any considerable variation in the substantive
complexity of the work: job conditions are not readily
modified to suit the needs or capacities of the individual

worker. Over a long enough time, though--certainly over a period as long as ten years--many men either modify their jobs or move on to other jobs more consonant with their intellectual functioning. Thus, the long-term effects of intellectual flexibility on substantive complexity are considerable, even though the contemporaneous effects appear to be negligible.

Our models, of course, start in mid- or later-career. There is every reason to believe that men's levels of intellectual flexibility in childhood, adolescence, and early adulthood may have had an important effect on their educational attainments, and our data show that educational attainment has had an extremely important effect on the substantive complexity of the early jobs in men's careers. Since the substantive complexity of early jobs is a primary determinant of the substantive complexity of later jobs, it seems safe to infer that intellectual flexibility's long-term, indirect effects on the substantive complexity of later jobs has been even greater than our analysis depicts.

In the broadest sense, our findings support our general strategy for studying the relationship between social structure and personality. We have consistently argued that, in interpreting the relationship between social structure and individual psychological functioning, one should always ask how a person's position in the larger social structure affects the conditions of life that directly impinge on him (see Kohn 1963, 1969, 1977; Kohn and Schooler 1969, 1973; Schooler 1972, 1976). Thus, in attempting to interpret the relationship between social class and values and orientation, we saw class-correlated differences in occupational conditions as a potentially important bridge between position in the hierarchical ordering of society and conceptions of reality (Kohn 1969; Kohn and Schooler 1969). Substantive complexity is particularly important for, on the one hand, the substantive complexity of work is closely linked to the job's location in the stratificational system and, on the other hand, the substantive complexity of people's work is correlated with their values and orientation. Our past research demonstrated that the relationship between social class and values and orientation could reasonably be attributed, in large degree, to class-correlated differences in such occupational conditions as substantive complexity. But not even our two-stage least squares analysis (Kohn and Schooler 1973) demonstrated conclusively that substantive complexity has an actual causal effect on values, orientation, or any other psychological phenomenon. The present analysis buttresses our analytic strategy by showing that substantive complexity actually does have a causal impact on one pivotal aspect of psychological functioning, intellectual flexibility.

Admittedly, our research has not yet demonstrated that substantive complexity directly affects values or self-conception or social orientation--in fact, anything other than intellectual flexibility. Still, intellectual flexibility is the crucial test. Because of its remarkable stability, intellectual flexibility offers the most difficult challenge to the hypothesis that substantive complexity actually affects some important aspect of psychological functioning. Moreover, intellectual flexibility is tremendously important in its own right. Finally, we see intellectual flexibility as intimately related to values, self-conception, and social orientation. It is, in fact, an important link between social class and self-directed values and orientation (Kohn 1969, pp. 186-7; Kohn and Schooler 1969). Thus, demonstrating the causal impact of substantive complexity on intellectual flexibility gives us every reason to expect substantive complexity to have a causal impact on values and orientation, too. In our further analyses, we shall assess the hypothesized causal impact of substantive complexity--and of other structural imperatives of the job--on values, self-conception, and social orientation. For now, one crucial causal link in the relationship between social structure and psychological functioning has been conclusively demonstrated.

References

Alwin, Duane F. 1973. "Making Inferences from Attitude-Behavior Correlations." Sociometry 36 (June): 253-78.

Baltes, Paul B. 1968. "Longitudinal and Cross-sectional Sequences in the Study of Age and Generation Effects." Human Development 11 (No. 3):131-90.

Burt, Ronald S. 1973. "Confirmatory Factor-Analytic Structures and the Theory Construction Process." Sociological Methods and Research 2 (November): 131-90.

Duncan, Otis Dudley. 1975. Introduction to Structural Equation Models. New York: Academic Press.

Heise, David R. 1975. Causal Analysis. New York: Wiley.

Joreskog, Karl G.   1969.   "A General Approach to
    Confirmatory Maximum Likelihood Factor Analysis."
    Psychometrika 34 (June):183-202.
------.   1973.   "A General Method for Estimating a
    Linear Structural Equation System."   Pp. 85-112
    in Structural Equation Models in the Social Sciences,
    edited by Arthur S. Goldberger and Otis Dudley
    Duncan.   New York: Seminar Press.
Joreskog, Karl G. and Sorbom,   D.   1976.   "Statistical
    Models and Methods for Analysis of Longitudinal Data."
    Pp. 285-325 in Latent Variables in Socioeconomic Models,
    edited by D. J. Aigner and A. S. Goldberger.   Amsterdam:
    North-Holland Publishing Co.
Joreskog, Karl G. and Marielle van Thillo.   1972.   "LISREL:
    A General Computer Program for Estimating a Linear
    Structural Equation System Involving Multiple Indicators
    of Unmeasured Variables."   Research Bulletin 72-56.
    Princeton, N. J.: Educational Testing Service.
Kohn, Melvin L.   1963.   "Social Class and Parent-Child
    Relationships: An Interpretation."   American Journal
    of Sociology 68 (January):471-80.
------.   1969.   Class and Conformity: A Study in Values.
    Homewood, Illinois: The Dorsey Press.   (Second Edition,
    1977, Published by the University of Chicago Press.)
------.   1976.   "Occupational Structure and Alienation."
    American Journal of Sociology 82 (July):111-30.
------.   1977.   "Reassessment, 1977."   Pp. xxv-lx in Melvin
    L. Kohn, Class and Conformity: A Study in Values.
    Second Edition.   Chicago: University of Chicago Press.
Kohn, Melvin L. and Carmi Schooler.   1969.   "Class, Oc-
    cupation and Orientation."   American Sociological
    Review 34 (October):659-78.
Kohn, Melvin L. and Carmi Schooler.   1973.   "Occupational
    Experience and Psychological Functioning: An Assessment
    of Reciprocal Effects."   American Sociological Review
    38 (February):97-118.
Rosenbaum, James E.   1976.   Making Inequality: The Hidden
    Curriculum of High School Tracking.   New York: John
    Wiley and Sons.
Schooler, Carmi.   1972.   "Social Antecedents of Adult
    Psychological Functioning."   American Journal of
    Sociology 78 (September):299-322.
------.   1976.   "Serfdom's Legacy: An Ethnic Continuum."
    American Journal of Sociology 81 (May):1265-86.
Sorbom, Dag.   1975.   "Detection of Correlated Errors in
    Longitudinal Data."   British Journal of Mathematical
    and Statistical Psychology 28:138-51.
Spaeth, Joe L.   1976.   "Characteristics of the Work Setting
    and the Job as Determinants of Income."   Pp. 161-76 in

Schooling and Achievement in American Society, edited by William H. Sewell, Robert M. Hauser, and David L. Featherman. New York: Academic Press.

Witkin, H. A., R. B. Dyk, H. F. Faterson, D. R. Goodenough and S. A. Karp. 1962. Psychological Differentiation: Studies of Development. New York: Wiley.

3

Aging and Social Support

Robert L. Kahn

As a social psychologist new to the topic of aging and life course, I have acquired in a relatively short time a fair amount of information and a large amount of humility -- both reflecting the inevitable naivete of a newcomer to a complicated and long-explored territory. Nevertheless, I would like to offer four impressions of past work on the subject of aging and life course, as a sort of preamble to describing some research that I hope may contribute to its future development.

The four impressions are quickly disposed of:

(1) The study of aging (growing up and growing old) has been marked by controversies over matters of substance and method, many of which fall on one side or the other of an ancient issue -- old age as defeat or as a kind of triumph. Thus, some researchers seek and sometimes find evidence for a long, inevitable decline in the later years. The categories of that decline supply the subheads for annual review articles -- decremental change in the central nervous system, in psychomotor responses, information processing, concept attainment and problem solving, learning and memory, perception, personality, and attitudes. Other research workers and many practitioners take an anti-decremental stance. They argue that the period of decline often comes very late, that the variance among older people is more impressive than the central tendency toward decrement, that there are offsetting gains on some dimensions, and that the more interesting and constructive research questions have to do with factors that prevent or offset decremental changes.

(2) Perhaps the single most prominent examples of these gerontological controversies is the argument over disengagement versus activity (or more recently, attachment) as the key concept for understanding aging, especially "successful" aging.

(3) Some agreement seems to be developing about the feasibility and advantage of describing aging more generally, in terms that are less "stage-specific" and more applicable to the life course as a whole.

(4) Finally, there is a need for what Lazarsfeld long ago called variable language -- meaning, of course, not language that varies but a language of quantitative variables rather than qualitative fixed types.

My colleagues and I at the Institute for Social Research (especially French, Quinn, Caplan and, until his recent move to Brown University, Sidney Cobb) have for some years been engaged in a program of research on the effects of the immediate social environment on health, especially mental health. Several aspects of this research seem relevant to the issues of aging to which I have referred:

(1) the relations of role characteristics, especially properties of the work role, to individual well-being;

(2) the refinement of those relationships in terms of person-environment fit, that is, goodness of fit between the needs and abilities of the individual on the one hand and, on the other, the supplies and demands of the environment as expressed in role expectations and perquisites;

(3) the importance of social support, both as a direct determinant of well-being and a buffer against the effects of stressful events.

As these points of emphasis suggest, our programmatic approach alters the traditional explanatory sequence in the field of mental health and illness. Most investigators have sought explanations of such phenomena in terms of individual vulnerability or strength, and have attempted to trace those characteristics to origins in past experience, childhood socialization, or genetic endowment. Properties of the contemporary adult environment then become sources of residual variance, unexplained and unwelcome.

We have attempted to reverse these priorities, and have sought first to discover how much of individual well-being or the lack of it can be explained by characteristics of the individual's immediate social environment - its demands, its opportunities, its support. Variance unexplained in these terms becomes the subject of investigations emphasizing personality, history, or genetics.

A similar distinction can be seen in the field of aging, between those investigators who seek characteristics of aging as such, purified of surrounding circumstances, and investigators whose first interest is to discover how much of what is usually called aging is determined by those same surrounding circumstances, physical and social.

In the remainder of this paper I will (1) offer some examples of research findings in each of the areas cited above - role, person-environment fit, and social support -- that seem relevant for aging; (2) propose a way of integrating these findings in terms of the concept of the <u>convoy of social support</u>; and (3) state as hypotheses some relationships between age, convoy characteristics, and well-being.

Role Stress and Well-Being

Studies of role stress are numerous, and there have been several recent reviews (Kahn and Quinn, 1970; Warr and Wall, 1975; McGrath, 1976). Most such studies have been done around the performance of tasks, either in the laboratory or on the job. One of the forms of stress identified early in such research was role conflict, that is, role expectations that are mutually incompatible with the individual's own values or beliefs about what is appropriate to the role. People subjected to such conflicts in the work role show various symptoms of dissatisfaction, emotional tension, and physical discomfort. Moreover, the experience of role conflict is common; it was reported by about half of the employed respondents in a national survey.

Later studies in the same program demonstrated that the single most common form of role conflict at work was overload -- pressure to do more work, inability to finish one's work in an ordinary day, and conflict between quantity and quality, the feeling that the amount of work interferes with "how well it gets done." These items correlated .6 with measures of tension and explain much of the effect that we had ascribed to role conflict in general.

In subsequent studies at two scientific installations of the federal government, French and Caplan (1973) concentrated on the issue of workload, and developed measures that included "underload" or underutilization as well as overload; they also distinguished between quantitative and qualitative load. The dimensions of measurement thus ran from "having too little to do" to "having too much to do," and from "having things that are too easy to do" to "having things that are too difficult to do."

Overload rather than underutilization, predictably enough, was the dominant experience in this population of scientists, engineers, and administrators; 73 per cent of them reported overload as a common experience. Both quantitative and qualitative overload were related to feelings of tension. Measures independent of self report corroborate these findings. Reported overload was consistent with the number of observed telephone calls and personal interruptions (r=.6), and both objective and subjective measures were correlated with heart rate (r=.4 and .7) and with cholesterol level (r=.4).

Caplan (1971) and Cobb (1974) took the question of workload still further, concentrating on responsibility as one kind of load, and distinguishing between responsibility for people and responsibility for things. Responsibility for people, and especially for people's futures, was related to such coronary risk factors as diastolic blood pressure, cholesterol level, and cigarette smoking among people who scored high on those measures of conscientiousness that Friedman and Rosenman have called marks of the "Type A personality" (Rosenman, et al., 1964). Cobb's review (1974) presents a number of occupational comparisons that are consistent with the interpretation of workload, especially responsibility for the future of others, as a source of stress. These occupational contrasts include anesthesiologists and general practioners as compared to dermatologists and pathologists, foremen as compared to craftsmen, and air traffic controllers as compared to second-class airmen. Criterion variables include coronary heart disease, hypertension, diabetes, and peptic ulcer. The pattern is persuasive.

Early studies in our program investigated role ambiguity as a source of stress parallel in some respects to role conflict. We conceived of role ambiguity as the discrepancy between the amount of information a person has and the amount needed to perform adequately in the role under study. We found reported role ambiguity to be prevalent in the work situation; about 33 per cent of employed respondents in a national survey said they were unclear about their responsibilities and were disturbed by that fact, and about equal numbers reported unclarity and disturbance about what their peers expected of them, how their supervisors evaluated them, and what their opportunities for advancement might be. The experience of ambiguity was correlated with job-related tension (.5), with a sense of futility (.4), and with low trust and liking for co-workers.

We have not attempted a differentiation of the ambiguity concept as we have the concept of role conflict, but it seems worth distinguishing between ambiguity about what is presently required of a person and ambiguity about the future. In the study of government scientists, engineers, and administrators, it is future ambiguity that accounts for most of the relationship with the affective criterion variables. To what extent conflict and ambiguity -- inconsistent and uncertain signals about present requirements, future events, and evaluation by significant others -- characterize different stages of the life course awaits investigations.

Person-Environment Fit

The idea that criteria of individual well-being could be predicted more accurately by taking properties of the situation and of the person simultaneously into account came early in our research. The relationship between role conflict and individual symptoms of strain was moderated substantially by such personality variables as flexibility-rigidity and introversion-extroversion. The stress effects of responsibility for others were apparent only among people of personality Type A -- the involved, striving, pressure-seekers.

French, Rodgers, and Cobb (1974) proposed a general model for dealing simultaneously with properties of the person and of the situation or environment in which the person is functioning. The key concept in the model is person-environment fit, that is, goodness of fit between the needs of the person and the supplies of the person's environment, and between the abilities of the person and the demands of the environment. The basic hypotheses are that misfit between these individual and situational characteristics will lead individuals to be dissatisfied with their roles, to be depressed, and to show other symptoms of strain and ill health. Whether the implied curves are symmetrical, that is, whether having too little and having too much are equally stressful, we have regarded as a question for exploration in a wide range of situations and variables.

Several studies of person-environment fit have now been completed, and the results have been summarized by Harrison (1976). The most ambitious of them (Caplan, et al., 1975) involved some 23 occupations and 2,000 men, several hundred of whom were randomly chosen as a subsample for the analyses of person-environment fit. The first such analysis concerned job complexity in relation to six criteria of strain -- dissatisfaction, boredom, somatic complaints, anxiety, depression, and irritation. In every case the measure of

goodness of fit adds significantly to the variance explained
by situational characteristics alone, personal characteristics alone, or both together.

The results are not equally straightforward for all situational factors, but they are equally plausible. Consider,
for example, the analysis of workload effects. Overload is
associated with symptoms of strain in all occupations, but
"underload" (underutilization) seems to evoke strain only
when the role is intrinsically rewarding. Thus, among administrators and scientists job dissatisfaction tends to be ele-
vated when there is too little work as well as when there is
too much. Among policemen and assembly-line workers, however,
the relationship between workload and satisfaction is linear
rather than curvilinear; that is, too much work is dissatis-
fying, but too little is not.

The study of person and environment in commensurate
terms has only begun, and extrapolation to the role of the
elderly in particular is hazardous. It is also tempting. I
believe that the "too little" end of many descriptive dimensions may be crucial for understanding the behavior and symptoms of many old people -- too little to do, too little responsibility, too little opportunity to exert influence or
to be of help.

Buffering Effect of Social Support

In our effort to understand the relationships between
specific situational stresses and specific indicators of
individual strain, we have sought interpersonal variables
that enter into those relationships. Among such variables
are mutual confidence and trust between the individual and
those with whom he or she interacts, the ability to exert
influence, and the obligation to respond to influence attempts. We have come to think of such variables as partial
measures of an underlying concept -- social support.

Cobb (1976), in a review paper of unusual range, and in
the subsequent chapter of this book, shows that social support buffers or protects people from some of the pathological
effects of many stressful life situations and transitions:
at birth, in infancy, during episodes of hospitalization and
recovery from illness, at times of job loss, and in bereavement. The buffering effects of social support are not
demonstrable in every case, but the general trend is strong.
Moreover, the measures of social support differ across studies, as do the criteria of strain: low birth weight, arthritis, tuberculosis, depression, alcoholism, amount of medication required for relief of symptoms, duration of illness,

and many others.

French (1974) had shown earlier that many, though not
all, of the stress-strain relationships in our own research
were moderated by social support. For example, the research
in government scientific installations showed a relationship
between role ambiguity and the level of serum cortisol in
the blood, an indicator of physiological strain; this relationship was eliminated, however, when relations between
supervisor and subordinates were supportive. Similar effects
occurred in the correlations between workload and such
criteria of physiological strain as blood pressure and serum
glucose levels. Again, however, not all measures of social
support showed this buffering effect, and not all stress-
strain relationships seemed to be buffered by the same kind
of social support.

Pinneau's (1975) more recent analysis of social support,
in the study of 2,000 men and 23 occupations to which I have
already referred, extends the mixed but intriguing pattern.
His results, granting the problems of inference from cross-
sectional data and self-report, show apparent direct effects
of social support on stress. Thus, when occupation and
other descriptors are held constant, men who reported supportive relations with their supervisors and co-workers also
reported less stress at work -- less role conflict, less
ambiguity, and the like. (Correlations range in the .30's
and .40's). Support from spouse and family shows a similar
but plausible weaker effect on work-generated stresses.

The data also show a consistent pattern of relationships
between social support and measures of psychological strain.
Partial correlations between support and the various strain
measures, with other significant predictors of strain held
constant, ranged from less than .2 to well above .4, with 33
out of 34 significant effects in the predicted direction.
Results within occupations were also consistent; social support was related (negatively) to depression, for example, in
15 out of 16 occupational groups. On the other hand, this
pattern of findings did not hold for the physiological
measures of strain, nor for the predicted interactions;
that is, evidence for the buffering effect was lacking.

Our experience to date with social support variables has
led us to two decisions of research strategy. First, in
studies of work situations and transitions we will continue
to investigate the forms of social support and the circumstances in which each is effective -- as a direct reducer
of stress and strain, and as a buffer or moderating variable
between stress and strain. Second, in a new series of

studies we propose to make the concept of social support central, to measure it in terms independent of self-report, and to study its effects in domains beyond the work role. We are especially interested in the possibility that social support may help explain certain phenomena of aging and life-course change.

The Convoy of Social Support*

The key concept that we propose for studying the process of aging and other life-course changes is the convoy. By choosing this metaphorical term we imply that each person can be thought of as moving through life surrounded by a set of significant other people to whom that person is related by giving or receiving of social support. An individual's convoy at any point in time thus consists of the set of persons on whom he or she relies for support and those who rely on him or her for support. These two subsets may overlap, of course; there are relationships in which one both gives and receives support, although not all relationships are symmetrical in this sense.

The implications of this conceptual approach can be summarized in terms of three general propositions, each of which identifies a category of more specific hypotheses:

(1) The adequacy of social support is a determinant of individual well-being, of performance in the major social roles, and of success in managing life-changes and transitions.

(2) The formal properties of a person's convoy determine the adequacy of the social support that person receives and has the opportunity to give.

(3) Demographic and situational variables -- age, sex, race, residence, and the like -- in turn determine the formal properties of a person's convoy.

In combination, these three hypotheses define a straightforward causal sequence -- from demographic characteristics to the structure of the convoy, from convoy

---

*I make no claims for having invented the idea of the convoy as a source of social support, but it is difficult to know whom to credit. Ralph Waldo Emerson used it in poetry many years ago; David Plath used it in a presentation to a committee of the Social Science Research Council in 1975. Robert Quinn and I have developed a research proposal in which the convoy is a central concept.

structure to the qualitative and quantitative adequacy of
social support, and from the adequacy of social support to
individual well-being or lack of it. A fourth hypothesis
involves the buffering effect of social support to moderate
the relationship between acute stresses (bereavements, imposed residential change, or job loss, for example) and
criteria of well-being. These four categories of hypotheses
are illustrated below:

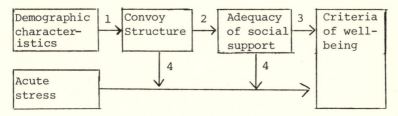

The Definition of Social Support

Social support is one of those terms that carries considerable colloquial meaning and is therefore more often used
than defined. Moreover, those who define social support do
so in various ways. We propose that social support be defined as interpersonal transactions that include one or more
of the following: the expression of positive affect of one
person toward another; the affirmation or endorsement of
another person's behaviors, perceptions, or expressed views;
the giving of symbolic or material aid to another. The key
elements in supportive transactions are thus _affect_, _affirma-
tion_, and _aid_.

By affective transactions we mean expressions of liking,
admiration, respect, or love. By transactions of affirmation
we mean expressions of agreement, or acknowledgement of the
appropriateness or rightness of some act or statement of
another person. Imagine, for example, two people leaving a
meeting together. One turns to the other for affirmation of
his own perceptions and interpretations of what really hap-
pened, who was in the right, what was left unsaid, and the
like. We go through life seeking meaning, and we depend on
the reactions of others for our construction of meaning out
of our own experience.

Finally, we include as social support those transactions
in which direct aid or assistance is given. This third element in the definition we include with some hesitation, because it admits too much. If the giving of material things,
money, information, time, and entitlements are all to be
called social support, the concept becomes too inclusive. We
do not wish to include every bureaucratic award of funds --

the sending of a Social Security check, for example, as <u>so-cial</u> support, although it is an obvious and important form of economic support. On the other hand, advice from an experienced worker to a novice about operating a balky machine seems to belong in the domain of social support. For the present, we prefer a broad conceptual definition, and will expect to restrict it somewhat by means of specific hypotheses and measures.

Convoys and Role Sets

The concept of the convoy and the related hypotheses have developed from many sources. Work on the life course, on social support, on the measurement of social networks, on the goodness-of-fit between individual and situational properties, and on role behavior are the most important of these. Because role concepts and role theory are well known, the convoy approach can be explicated in terms of its similarities and differences to role theory. The writings of G.H. Mead, Talcott Parsons, and Robert Merton share an emphasis on the explanation of human behavior in terms of social roles, in which each person interacts with and responds to certain significant others.

Like the role set (Merton, 1957), the convoy consists of an individual and a set of other people defined in terms of their relationship to that individual. The convoy differs from the role set, however, in that it is defined by the giving and receiving of social support rather than by a person's position in a formal organization, family, or other social structure. Role theory begins by partitioning the life of an individual into its positional or organizational components; the convoy begins by locating, for a given individual, all those other persons with whom there is a significant pattern of support-giving or receiving. The transactions of giving and receiving support cut across positions and roles.

A second major difference between role research and the proposed research on convoys involves the relative emphasis on static versus dynamic issues. Whether or not the role concept is inherently static, role research has tended to concentrate on static questions; different work roles have been compared, for example, with respect to the stresses they impose and the satisfaction they provide. The concept of the convoy, on the other hand, implies movement; a person who has a convoy is going some place. The movement of interest varies, of course, depending on the problem we wish to understand. It may be a particular transition -- for example, a movement from school to work, a change of jobs, a

retirement, or a geographical relocation. And in some cases
we may wish to concentrate on changes in the convoy itself.
Divorce or the death of a spouse, for example, can be studied
in these terms.

Finally, the convoy differs from the role set in its
emphasis on the giving as well as the receiving of social
support. Role theory has typically been concerned with
transmittal in one direction, the sending of role expectations from members of the role set to the focal person. The
elements of the convoy, on the other hand, form a set defined
both by giving and receiving of social support in relation
to the focal person. The integration of the convoy model
with role theory is a possibility worth pursuing, but the
pursuit lies beyond the limits of this paper.

Formal Properties of Convoys

The research utility of the convoy depends in part on
the specification and measurement of its formal properties.
These can best be regarded as consisting of two subsets, properties of the convoy as a whole, and properties of the separate dyadic links between the focal person and each of the
convoy members. The following two listings are partial, and
both owe much to Barnes' (1972) work on network analysis:

Properties of the convoy as a whole

Size - number of persons defined as members

Internal connectedness - proportion of convoy
   members who are acquainted with each other,
   or who are related to each other directly
   through support-giving or receiving.

External connectedness - number of convoy members
   who are related to specific categories of other
   persons (e.g., community influentials, organization executives)

Homogeneity - similarities among members

Stability - average duration of membership

Symmetry - proportion of relationships that
   are both support-giving and support-receiving

Properties of dyadic links within convoys

Frequency - number of transactions per unit of

time (e.g., month)

Magnitude - importance of transactions

Initiative - number and proportion of transactions
    initiated by focal person and by others; perhaps
    also the potential for initiation by each

Range - number of life domains included in
    transactions (e.g., family, work, neighbor-
    hood)

Type - transactions involving affective expression,
    affirmation, or direct assistance as dominant
    content

Symmetry - relationship primarily support-giving,
    support-receiving, or both

Duration - time since inception of the relationship

Capacity - maximum potential support under
    specified circumstances

As graph theory develops, especially in application to
social networks, we may hope that a logically complete set of
network properties will be specified. For the present, any
list of such properties must be open-ended, generated in part
from formal sources, but in part also from intuitive notions
about the giving and receiving of social support, and about
the relationships within which such transactions occur.

Aging and Social Support

Two lines of inquiry seem promising here, one exploratory and one predictive. The question to be explored is how
the convoy characteristics, and the giving and receiving of
social support, typically change with age, from birth to
death. I suppose it is obvious that the infant is in need of
support of many kinds from the moment of birth and that the
infant can give few kinds of support in return -- although
the immediate emotional rewards of parenthood may be very
great. The convoy characteristics of old age are less obvious, but we would expect them to include the following:
increasing asymmetry (receiving without having the opportunity to give), reduced initiative (ability to initiate interaction rather than await it), increased instability (loss of
convoy members), reduced convoy size (because of loss without
opportunity for replacement), and changes in type of interaction (relatively less receiving of affect and affirmation,

and increases in some forms of direct aid).

In a preliminary study of about 300 adults of all ages in one community, Robert Quinn and I collected data about convoy structure by means of survey interviews. People found the questions meaningful, and some age-related data emerged. The size of the convoy increases during the years of young adulthood and is quite stable during the years from 35 to 55. The pattern of affective expression did not decrease within this age range, but the receiving of aid and assistance in various forms increased with age.

The limited sample size prevented differentiation of the age group beyond 55 in this preliminary study, but other research shows significant changes around the age of 70 that we would attempt to explain partly as changes in convoy characteristics. For example, a nationwide study of the sub- jective quality of life (Campbell, Converse, and Rodgers, 1976) shows greater overall life satisfaction among people in their 60's than in their 50's, but a decline after age 70. The same pattern appears in a number of the specific life domains, although not in all. Satisfaction with health de- clines steadily from the time of young adulthood, with a large difference between the responses of people in their 50's and those in their 60's.

Some of our predictions have less to do with these gen- eral trends than with deviations from them. For example, we expect that elderly people with relatively large convoy numbers and more nearly symmetrical relationships will also show relatively "youthful" characteristics on the criterion dimensions of role performance and experienced quality of life. Some characteristics conventionally ascribed to aging, in other words, we expect to be able to explain in part as changes in the convoy pattern.

Should such predictions hold, they should be made the subject of field experiments. Even if measures of well-be- ing are related to convoy properties and to the pattern of social support, some obvious problems of causal inference remain. Properties of the convoy may determine well-being, but people may also choose their convoys and define their relationships to convoy members. The experimental enlarge- ment of convoys and supportive relationships will test our preferred hypotheses and the plausible alternatives. Such experiments may also suggest policies that can enhance the experience of aging, in particular the experience of growing old in our society.

References

Barnes, J.A. Social networks. New York: Addison-Wesley
   Reprints, 1972.

Campbell, A., Converse, P.E. and Rodgers, W.L. 1976. The
   Quality of American life. New York: Russell Sage Foundation.

Caplan, R.D. 1971. Organizational stress and individual
   strain: a socio-psychological study of risk factors in
   coronary heart disease among administrators, engineers,
   and scientists (doctoral dissertation, University of Michigan). Dissertation Abstracts International, 1972, 32,
   6706b-6707b (University Microfilms, 72-14822).

Caplan, R.D., Cobb, S., French, J.R.P., Jr., Harrison, R.D.
   and Pinneau, S.R., Jr. 1975. Job demands and worker
   health: main effects and occupational differences. Washington, D.C.: U.S. Government Printing Office.

Cobb, S. 1976. Social support as a moderator of life stress.
   Psychosomatic Medicine, Vol. 3, 5, 300-314.

Cobb, S. 1974. Role responsibility: the differentiation of a
   concept. In McLean, A. (Ed.) Occupational Stress.
   Springfield, Ill.: Thomas.

French, J.R.P., Jr., 1974. Person-Role Fit. In McLean, A. (Ed.)
   Occupational Stress. Springfield, Ill.: Thomas.

French, J.R.P., Jr., 1973. Organizational stress and individual strain. In Marrow, A.J. (Ed.) The failure of success.
   New York: Amacom (American Management Association).

French, J.R.P., Jr., Rodgers, W.L. and Cobb, S. 1974. Adjustment as person-environment fit. In Coelho, G., Hamburg, D.
   and Adams, J. (Eds.) Coping and adaptation. New York:
   Basic Books.

Harrison, R.V. 1976. Job demands and worker health: person-
   environment misfit   (doctoral dissertation, University
   of Michigan). Dissertation Abstracts International, 1976,
   37, 1035B; University Microfilms 76-19150).

Kahn, R.L. and Quinn, R.P. 1970. Role stress: a framework
   for analysis. In McLean, A. (Ed.) Mental health and work
   organizations. Chicago: Rand McNally.

McGrath, J.E. 1976. Stress and behavior in organizations. In Dunnette, M.D. (Ed.) Handbook of industrial and organizational psychology. Chicago: Rand McNally.

Merton, R.K. 1957. Social theory and social structure, Rev. ed. New York: Fress Press.

Pinneau, S.R., Jr. Effects of social support on psychological and physiological strains. Doctoral dissertation. University of Michigan, 1975.

Rosenman, R.H., et al. 1964. A predictive study of coronary heart disease. Journal of the American Medical Association, 189, 15-26.

Warr, P. and Wall, T. 1975. Work & well-being. Baltimore: Penguin Books.

Social Support and Health Through the Life Course

Sidney Cobb

All the world's great religions support the Golden Rule in one form or another. "Love thy neighbor as thyself," (Leviticus XIX 18) has been the advice of our spiritual leaders for many centuries. Only lately have those of us concerned with health come to realize the importance of this kind of prescription. We tend to call this social support and to fit it into a general notion of support systems. In this essay I shall attempt to do three things: explain what social support is and where it fits in a broader scheme of support systems, summarize the rather overwhelming literature relating this concept to various aspects of health, and discuss a possible theoretical explanation for the way in which social support acts to promote the health of individuals.

The Nature of Social Support

There are four kinds of support. The first and most important is social support. It is sometimes called communicated caring. It is purely informational in nature and it has three components. (1) Emotional support leading the recipient to believe that she is cared for and loved. (2) Esteem support leading the recipient to believe that she is esteemed and valued. (3) Network support leading the recipient to believe that she has a defined position in a network of communication and mutual obligation.

The second form of support is instrumental support or counseling. This involves guiding persons to better coping and/or adaptation and to maximization of their participation and autonomy.

The third is active support or mothering. This is what mothers do for infants and nurses do for patients. When done unnecessarily it may lead to dependency.

The fourth is material support or goods and services. This is the equivalent of Kahn's "aid," as in the previous chapter. The provision of goods and technical services might be thought to include active support. The distinction can be made clear by the example of an overworked executive. On the one hand, if his boss comes and does part of the job for him, it comes under the rubric of active support and can fit into the sequence of mothering-smothering-spoiling. On the other hand, if the boss permits the executive to hire himself an assistant and/or buy a piece of equipment to expedite his work, it comes under material support.

It is important to note that instrumental support, active support, and material support may involve or imply social support. For example, taking the time to counsel a student may communicate that you care. In feeding a special meal to her grown son, a mother communicates love as well as providing nourishment. In giving a student a scholarship, one communicates esteem as well as providing money. Because of this confounding the focus of any support system will always appear to be on social support. This is important as a source of bias in research, but is probably entirely appropriate for it is my belief that social support is more important than all the others put together. (Cobb, 1976)

With this view of the position of social support, let us examine its components in more detail. Emotional support is information that one is cared for and loved or, as the Greeks might say, information about agapé. It is transmitted in intimate situations involving mutual trust. In a dyadic relationship this information meets Murray et al.'s (1938) need succorance for one person, need nurturance for the other, and need affiliation for both. This is part of what Kahn has called positive affect in the preceding chapter.

Information that one is valued and esteemed is most effectively proclaimed in public. It leads the individual to esteem himself and reaffirms his sense of personal worth, and above all it assures him of a personal and separate identity. It is called esteem support, and includes what Kahn has called affirmation.

Information that one has a place in a network of communication and mutual obligation must be common and shared. It must be common in the sense that everyone in the network has the information and shared in the sense that each member is aware that every other member knows. The relevant information is of three kinds. The first is historical. A strong network has a history. Kahn's use of

the word "convoy" is appropriate. The second pertains to
goods and services that are available to any member on
demand, and includes information about the accessibility of
services that are only occasionally needed--e.g. equipment,
specialized skills, technical information. The third
contains information that is common and shared with respect
to the dangers of life and the procedures for mutual defense.
In this last sense the knowledge that a competently staffed
hospital is available in case of need is socially supportive.

Social Support and Health

The effects of social support on health will be looked
at in several categories: the effects during pregnancy, the
effects on learning and early development, the effects on
health at the time of various life crises, the relationship
to various specific illnesses plus its effect on compliance
with prescribed medical regimens, and its general life
sparing effect.

During Pregnancy

With regard to the complications of pregnancy, Nuckolls
(1972) has shown that there is an interaction between life
change score and social support in the prediction of the
proportion who will have one or another complication of
pregnancy. My recalculation of her data shows that the
interaction is significant and that 91 percent of those with
a lot of life changes and low social support ended up with
complications compared to 43 percent of the other three
categories.

In addition to this there is some evidence that mothers
with unwanted pregnancies are likely to have smaller babies
than mothers who desired the pregnancy in the first place.
The principal observation in this area comes from a study by
Morris et al. in 1977. Curiously the findings are true both
for blacks and whites, but only for those with at least a
high school education. These findings were not confirmed by
Hultin and Ottosson (1971) in Sweden but their analyses did
not control for educational level of the mother. It is, of
course, not reasonable to suppose that "wantedness" is
information that is transmitted from mother to fetus and
thus influences growth rate; rather is seems likely that a
woman "rejects" her baby and functions less effectively as a
mother because she is herself inadequately socially supported. The societal reaction to illegitimate pregnancy is a
case in point. These two studies of birth weight did not
look at concomitant environmental stresses, and one of them

suffers from the disadvantage of being a retrospective inquiry.

In Early Development

The first real adaptive demand that is placed on the child is the achievement of sphincter control. Stein and Susser (1967) report that bladder control at night was significantly delayed for those children whose mothers went out to work while the children were in the second six months of life. This was not true if the mother went out to work earlier or later. Two studies of the children of mothers who requested abortion but had those abortions refused (reported by Forssman and Thuwe, 1966, and Dytrych et al., 1975) both suggest, but neither really proves, that wanted children adapt to and/or cope with the stresses of growing up better than those who started out with parental request for abortion that was denied. The thrust of significant results of these two studies seems to be in the socialization area. Particularly striking was the lesser educational achievement of the unwanted children as compared to the controls. These studies, one done in Scandinavia and the other in Czechoslovakia, deserve to be replicated in this country now that abortions are more available.

In Life Transitions and Crises

The next area of concern is the transition to adult life. There are obvious stresses associated with the first job and with the beginning of marital and family responsibilities, but there seems to be little in the way of data about the effect of social support at the time of this transition. Research in this area is clearly indicated. Elsewhere (Cobb and Kasl, 1977) I have examined the effects of social support in moderating the consequences of job termination. The effects are striking with respect to most of the psychological variables, but with respect to the physiological variables examined the effects were only of border line significance. However, when it came to the disease category of arthritis, there was a tenfold increase in the frequency of joint swelling as one moved from the highest third of social support to the lowest.

Erikson (1976) has written eloquently of his observations in the case of the Buffalo Creek flood which destroyed so many homes. He makes it clear that, from an observational standpoint at least, social support was an important variable. However, his most telling comments bear on the extent to which support networks were destroyed by the newly developed housing arrangements and the consequences of this loss of network support.

Weiss (1975) has noted the importance of social support for those going through a divorce, and many authors have noted the importance of social support under the stress of war (Rose, 1956; Mandelbaum, 1952; Titmuss, 1950; Swank, 1949; Reid, 1947). Menninger (1947), describing his World War II experiences, said, "We seemed to learn anew the importance of group ties in the maintenance of mental health."

As old age approaches, infirmity begins, and retirement takes place, further stresses occur. Much informal information has been published about the importance of social support at this time of life but there is relatively little hard evidence. Blau (1973) and Lowental and Haven (1968) present evidence that is at least suggestive that depression at this time of life is less frequent among those who are adequately socially supported. This, of course, is not a novel finding for, as will be seen in the next section, there is evidence that social support is protective with respect to depression throughout life.

Table 1. The Relationship of Perceived Social Support to Health Status of Women 13 Months After the Death of Their Husbands (Raphael, 1977).

Perceived Social Support	Reported Health at 13 Months			Percent Poor
	Good	Poor	Total	
1. Adequate	115	33	148	22
2. Inadequate	2	12	14	86
3. Inadequate-- "Treated"	14	2	16	13

$$1 \text{ vs } 2 \quad x^2 = 25.6, \ P < 0.001$$

$$2 \text{ vs } 3 \quad x^2 = 13.3, \ P < 0.001$$

When we come to bereavement the evidence is less strong than one might expect, for most of us act as though the bereavement period were a period requiring social support. Parkes (1972) and Burch (1972) present suggestive evidence. The data of Gerber et al. (1975) bear more directly on the subject but are disappointing in their presentation. They are at least suggestive of effects in the predicted direction. However, Raphael (1977) has presented striking evidence that those with little social support are more likely to report poor health thirteen months after bereavement than are those with more adequate support. Furthermore, he is able to demonstrate that supportive treatment for those with little social support leads to a return to the normal state of affairs at thirteen months. See Table 1.

In Specific Illnesses

Having skimmed the life course and shown effects at almost every stage, it is time to turn to some specific diseases. The relationship to diseases is of two sorts. First, there are associations of lack of social support with onset of the disease: e.g., tuberculosis reviewed by Chen and Cobb (1960), depression (Brown and his associates 1975 + 1977), arthritis (Cobb + Kasl, 1977), and coronary heart disease, noted by many authors in many ways (Caplan, 1971) but most notably by Parkes (1969) in his article entitled "The Broken Heart" in which he discusses the excess of coronary deaths among those men who have recently lost their wives. Second, there is evidence that recovery from cardiac failure (Chambers and Reiser, 1953), tuberculosis (Holmes et al., 1961), surgical operation (Egbert et al., 1964), asthma (deAraujo et al., 1973), psychosomatic illness (Berle et al., 1952), and various psychiatric illnesses (Lambert, 1973; Caplan, 1974; Hermalin, 1976; Brown, 1959) is accelerated or facilitated by high levels of social support.

In Compliance with Treatment

Part of this facilitation of recovery is mediated by improved compliance. It is an interesting and little known fact that the association of compliance and social support is one of the best documented relationships in all of medical sociology. Specifically, if a physician wants a patient to follow a complex routine for the maintenance of his health, as in hypertension, it is almost essential that he pay attention to the support systems in the patient's life. The literature in this area is summarized in two separate reviews (Baekeland and Lundwall, 1975; Haynes and Sackett, 1974). Of 41 articles, 34 support the association with compliance, 6 give insignificant results and 1 reports a negative finding. The association of lung cancer with cigarette smoking at the time of the Surgeon General's report was hardly stronger than that and yet this is an almost entirely neglected aspect of medical practice.

In Sparing Life

In the end one always gets involved with matters of life and death, and it is appropriate here to call attention to two important findings. The first has come to be known as the "Phillips effect." In a truly remarkable paper, Phillips and Feldman (1973) demonstrated in five separate studies that deaths are reduced in the six months preceding birthdays and increased in the succeeding six months. A summary of their data is presented in Figure 1. They went on to hypothesize that, if this were a social support effect, it should be more striking for the most distinguished people. They found this hypothesis to be dramatically confirmed.

The second important study was reported by Berkman at the last annual meeting of the American Public Health Association (1977). She provided data from the California Human Population Laboratory study of 7,000 residents of Alameda County which show that, over a ten year period, age adjusted mortality is reduced among those who have good network support. The support was measured in advance by 1) marriage, 2) contact with close friends and relatives, 3) church membership, 4) informal and formal group associations. There were successive decreases in age adjusted mortality rates for each of the four levels of social support for both males and females. The effect was independent of, and in addition to, the effect of positive health practices as reported by Belloc (1973). The risk of dying more than doubled from the highest to the lowest category of network support. We will all look forward with interest to the final publication of the detailed analyses of this important phenomenon.

Interpretations and Implications

Some of the effects of social support appear to be direct or main effects and others appear as interactions with stresses in the social environment. In my view it is not worth worrying about the distinction between main effects and interaction effects, for several reasons. The first is that few if any lives are entirely free of social and psychological stress so, when main effects appear, it may be that unmeasured stresses are producing an interaction effect that is large enough to appear also as a main effect. The second point is that it is quite reasonable to imagine that at very low levels of social support the deprivation would be strong enough to be a stress in itself, while at medium levels it would take some other environmental stress to highlight the deficit, and at the highest levels protection from strain might be very substantial. This notion is displayed graphically in Figure 2.

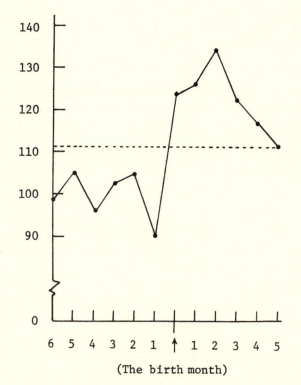

(The birth month)

Figure 1.   Number of deaths before, during,
and after birth month.   (Redrawn
from data of Phillips and Feldman
1973 reproduced with permission)

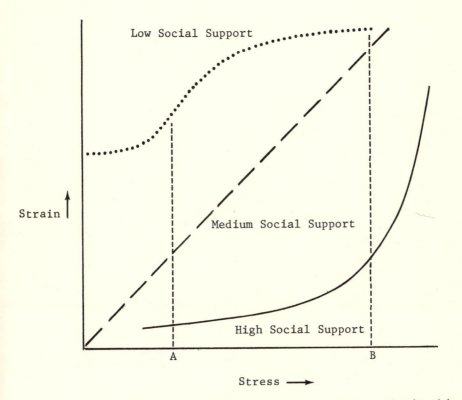

Figure 2.   An hypothesis about the nature of the relationship of stress and strain in the face of varying levels of social support.

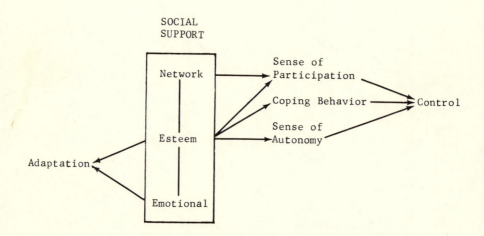

Figure 3. An hypothesis about the mechanism through which social support might operate to improve an individual relationship with the environment, thereby reducing psychosocial stress and thus relieving strain.

The implications of this theory are very interesting because they include the prediction that the interaction effect would look quite different for a dichotomy between high and medium than for the dichotomy between medium and low levels of social support. This would be especially true if the range of stress measured were limited, say from A to B in the diagram. If this formulation is correct, we should not be worried about main effects vs. interaction effects but should rather be concerned with mapping the three-dimensional relationship among the variables.

When it comes to thinking about the mechanism involved, it seems unlikely that social support could operate directly on so many indications of strain. It makes more sense to hypothesize that it operates to facilitate stress reduction by improving the fit between the person and the environment (French et al., 1975). The hypothesis is displayed in Figure 3. The three components of social support are located in the box in the middle of the figure. The arrows from Esteem Support and Emotional Support to Adaptation indicate the belief that those who are esteemed, therefore self confident, and those who are emotionally supported, therefore comfortable, are more able to change themselves to fit into a changed environment. Similarly, those who are confident have a sense of autonomy and are more likely to engage in coping behavior, and so are more likely to take control of their environments and to manipulate these environments into a more acceptable shape. By the same token, Network Support and Esteem Support contribute to a sense of participation in decision making, which likewise contributes to environmental control, or at least to the "illusion of control" which Perlmuter and Monty (1977) have shown may be as important as actual control.

In summary, social support, defined as the sum of emotional support, esteem support, and network support, has beneficial effects on a wide variety of health variables throughout the life course from conception to just before death, and on the bereaved who are left behind after a death. There are many faults in the various studies, but the repetitive nature of the effects using varied techniques is impressive. The pervasiveness of these social support effects suggests that we are dealing with a very general phenomenon and a really fundamental variable. One cannot escape the conclusion that the world would be a healthier place if training in supportive behavior were built into the routines of our homes and schools, and support worker roles were institutionalized.

References

Baekeland F, Lundwall L. 1975: Dropping out of treatment: a critical review. Psychol Bull 82:738-783

Belloc N. 1973: Relationship of health practices in mortality. Preventive Medicine 2:67-81

Berkman LF. 1977: Psychosocial resources health behavior and mortality; a nine year follow-up study. Read before APHA October 31, 1977

Berle BB, Pinsky RH, Wolf S, Wolf HG. 1952: Berle index: a clinical guide to prognosis in stress disease. J Am Med Assoc 149:1624-1628

Brown GW. 1959: Social factors influencing length of hospital stay of schizophrenic patients. Br Med J 2:1300-1302

Brown GW, Bhrolchain MN, Harris T. 1975: Social class and psychiatric disturbance among women in an urban population. Sociology 9:225-254

Brown GW, Davidson S, Harris T et al. 1977: Psychiatric disorder in London and North Uist. Soc Sci & Med 11:367-377

Burch J. 1972: Recent bereavement in relation to suicide J Psychosom Res 16:361-366

Caplan RD. 1971: Organizational stress and individual strain. Doctoral dissertation, University of Michigan

Caplan G. 1974: Support Systems and Community Mental Health. New York, Behavioral Publications

Chambers WN, Reiser MF. 1953: Emotional stress in the precipitation of congestive heart failure. Psychosom Med 15:38-60

Chen E, Cobb S. 1960: Family structure in relation to health and disease. J. Chron Dis 12:544-567

Cobb S. 1976: Social support as a moderator of life stress. Psychosom Med 38:300-314

deAraujo G, van Arsdel PP, Holmes TH, Dudley DL. 1973: Life change, coping ability and chronic intrinsic asthma. J Psychosom Res 17:359-363

Dytrych Z, Matejcek Z, Schüller V, David HP, Friedman HL. 1975: Children born to women denied abortion. Fam Plann Perspect 7:165-171

Egbert LD, Battit GE, Welch CE, Bartlett MK. 1964: Reduction of post-operative pain by encouragement and instruction of patients. N Eng J Med 270:825-827

Erikson KT. 1976: Everything in Its Path: Distruction of the Community in the Buffalo Creek Flood. New York. Simon and Schuster

Forssman H, Thuwe I. 1966: One hundred and twenty children born after application for therapeutic abortion refused. Acta Psychiatr Scand 42:71-88

French JRP Jr, Rodgers W, Cobb S. 1974: Adjustment as person-
    environment fit, in Coelho GV, Hamburg DA, Adams JE,
    Coping and Adaptation, New York, Basic Books
Gerber I, Wiener A, Battin D, Arkin A. 1975: Brief therapy
    to the aged bereaved, in Bereavement: Its Psychosocial
    Aspects, (edited by B. Schoenberg et al.). New York,
    Columbia University Press
Haynes RB, Sackett DL. 1974: A Workshop/Symposium:
    Compliance with Therapeutic Regimens--Annotated Bibliog-
    raphy. Department of Clinical Epidemiology and Biosta-
    tistics, McMaster University Medical Centre, Hamilton,
    Ontario
Hermalin JA. 1976: A predictive study of schizophrenic
    patient rehospitalization. Doctoral Dissertation, Brown
    University, Providence, Rhode Island
Holmes TH, Joffe JR, Ketcham JW et al. 1961: Experimental
    study of prognosis. J Psychosom Res 5:235-252
Hultin M, Ottosson MO. 1971: Perinatal conditions of
    unwanted children. Acta Pschiatr Scand (Suppl) 221:59-76
Lambert K. 1973: Agapé as a therapeutic factor in analysis.
    J Anal Psychol 18:25-46
Lowenthal ME, Haven C. 1968: Interaction and adaptation:
    intimacy as a critical variable. Am Sociol Rev 33:20-30
Mandelbaum DG. 1952: Soldier Groups and Negro Soldiers.
    Berkeley University of California Press. Edited by
    Bovard EW. Psychol Rev 66:267-277
Menninger WC. 1947: Psychiatric experience in the war 1941-
    1946. Am J Psychiatry 103:587-593
Morris NM, Udry JR, Chase CL. 1973: Reduction of low birth
    weight rates by prevention of unwanted pregnancies. Am
    J Pub Health 63:935-938
Murray HA et al. 1938: Explorations in Personalty. New York,
    Oxford University Press
Nuckolls KB, Cassel J, Kaplan BH. 1972: Psychosocial assets,
    life crisis and the prognosis of pregnancy. Am J
    Epidemiol 95:431-441
Parkes CM. 1972: Studies of Grief in Adult Life. New York,
    International Universities Press
Parkes CM, Benjamin B, Fitzgerald RG. 1969: Broken heart: a
    study of increased mortality among widowers. British
    Medical Journal 1:740-743
Perlmuter LC, Monty RA. 1977: The importance of perceived
    control: fact or fantasy? Am Scientist 65:759-765
Phillips DP, Feldman KA. 1973: A dip in deaths before
    ceremonial occasions: some new relationships between
    social integration and mortality. Am Soc Rev 38:678-696
Raphael B. 1977: Preventive intervention with the recently
    bereaved. Arch Gen Psychiatry 34:1450-1454

Reid DD. 1947: Some measures of the effect of operational stress on bomber crews, in Great Britain Air Ministry, Psychological Disorders in Flying Personnel of the R.A.F. London, His Majesty's Stationery Office

Rose AM. 1956: Factors in mental breakdown in combat, in Mental Health and Mental Disorder--A Sociological Approach (edited by AM Rose). London, Routledge and Kegan Paul

Stein Z, Susser M. 1967: Social factors in the development of sphincter control. Dev Med Child Neurol 9:692-706

Swank RL. 1949: Combat exhauston: a descriptive and statistical analysis of causes, symptoms and signs. J Nerv Ment Dis 109:475-508

Titmuss RH. 1950: Problems of Social Policy. London H.N. Stationery Office

Weiss RS. 1975: Marital separation, New York Basic Books

Part II

Aging and Social Change

Aging, Social Change and Social Policy

Matilda White Riley

At this moment in historical time, social change is affecting our lives from birth to death with perhaps special force. At both these anchor points there are signs of the alterations surrounding us. Biomedical technology and the demographic revolution have combined to make both birth and death increasingly salient: infant death has been sharply reduced in the United States at the same time that the pro- portion of all deaths occurring in the later years has been sharply increased. In the birthing process, the sterile loneliness of the delivery room, the use of mechanized inter- ventions and pain-reducing drugs, the rapid separation of mother and child seem to be gradually giving way to more "natural" settings and self-induced relaxation, often supported by the physical presence of the father of the child-to-be. Similarly, in the process of dying, increasing numbers of terminal elderly patients are expressing a desire to die at home, or in a hospice or some similar setting, where relatives and close friends are welcome, not rejected by hospital rules. In each instance, there are fresh emphases upon human interaction, upon the "social convoys" discussed in the chapters by Kahn and by Cobb.

What, then, is the impact of such social changes on the potential of the neonate to respond, to develop? On the old person's potential to face death, to resolve old problems, to cope with new ones? What is the impact of the many social changes that can be identified and examined as impinging upon each of the life-course phases intervening between birth and death?

The subsequent chapters in PART TWO of this symposium begin to approach such questions. They take up the challenge of PART ONE: to discover and uncover human potential over the full lifetime, and in particular to reject the dogma that growing old is a fixed and dismal process--ineluctable and

irreversible--and necessarily decremental. They press this
challenge by elaborating aspects of the relationship between
aging and social change. Thus these chapters move from a
primary focus on the aging of individuals, to explore the
linkages between aging and social change. They move from the
first set of premises formulated in my "Introduction"--that
aging is life-long and composed of interacting social, psychological, and biological processes, to my second set of
premises--that aging is influenced by, and in turn influences,
social change.

In this chapter, I shall provide further background for
understanding the linkages between the changing life course
of individuals and related changes in the society. Then I
shall emphasize the importance of such understanding as a
powerful tool for social policy.

Aging and Social Change

The notion of age refers not only to the micro-level
processes of individual aging from birth to death. At the
macro-level, the notion of age also has further referents: to
age norms in the changing social structure; and to the flow
of cohorts through the changing society. The successive
cohorts fit together at any given time to form age strata of
people who are young, middle aged, and old, and who are all
variously interacting with one another.

While such multiform meanings of age may seem familiar
enough, they are still elusive. Least familiar is the concept of cohort flow, probably because we ourselves are
"cohort-centric," blindfolded by the generation to which each
of us belongs. To be sure, students in introductory courses
in sociology or psychology are repeatedly told that, in every
society, infants are like small "barbarians" and must be
socialized. Yet students are rarely taught that each society
(and each of its institutions) is literally throbbing with
repeated invasions of barbarians requiring socialization
throughout their lives as they move from one role to another
up until death. Norman Ryder (1965)--along with such others
as Karl Mannheim (1928) and Pitirim Sorokin (1941)--were
among the first to dramatize the implications of some
of these principles, which now form the conceptual model for
the newly emerging sociology of age (Riley, Johnson, and
Foner, 1972; Riley, 1976).

In relating aging and social change, this model points
to two types of change that occur together. First, people in
the society are growing older (aging) and cohorts are dying
off and replacing one another. Second and simultaneously,

the society is changing--roles and institutions change;
historical events occur; science, beliefs, and values are
transformed; and the age structure of the population changes.
Hence, there are two different dynamisms: aging--or the
full life-course experience of cohorts as they are born and
follow one another through the society--and social change.
And these two sets of changes not only interpenetrate, they
are mutually dependent. To state this another way, social
change can take place only as the people in different cohorts
age in different ways. All too often in the past aging has
been viewed as involving fixed "life stages"--a notion that
is sharply challenged if not dispelled in this symposium.
Nor is the argument abstract or arcane. A moment's reflection shows that, as long as the life course is fixed--as
long as each cohort repeats the same life-course pattern as
its predecessors--there can be no social change (Ryder, 1972).

Synopsis of PART TWO

The remaining chapters in this book reflect this interdependence between social change and the ways in which successive cohorts age. Taken together, these chapters illustrate the nature of this interdependence, re-emphasizing the
central fact that this is a two-way process.

There is already wide awareness of one direction of this
process: that aging and cohort flow are in part caused by
changes in the society. Many cohort differences are understood as resulting from, or manifesting, social change. For
example, cohorts born recently differ from earlier cohorts
because of changes in education, in nutrition, in the income
level at which people began their careers, in the stock
market averages affecting pensions and retirement programs,
or in the political Zeitgeist surrounding people's first
voting experience.

The reciprocal process, that aging and cohort flow can
also cause social change, is less widely recognized, however.
Yet distinctive features of the particular cohorts themselves
can also react upon society to alter it. Noteworthy here is
the fact that a cohort is not merely an aggregate of individual biographies. It also constitutes a higher level of the
social system, with properties of its own. For example, each
cohort has a characteristic size--consider the well-known
effects of the size of the baby boom cohort on housing,
schools, or the labor market. Each cohort also has a distinctive composition--consider how the sex composition changes
over the life course of the cohort until its oldest members
are mostly women, with untold consequences both for them and
society. Average longevity is another cohort characteristic,

and the increasing longevity of successive cohorts over this
century has contributed to the literal transformation of the
structure of the kinship network. Moreover, each cohort
has unique experiences; thus the revolt of the student
cohort of the 1960's not only ignited public opinion against
the Vietnam War, but has also left its mark on many aspects
of popular taste.

From the societal standpoint, then, the study of age
is a study of changing people and their changing social roles.

The Method of Cohort Analysis

These conceptions of the sociology of age have their
counterpart in the method of cohort analysis, a powerful
tool for both research and, as I shall indicate later, for
policy planning. By cohort analysis, I mean the simple
mapping and direct comparison of pertinent information about
the life-course experiences of successive cohorts. In
research, cohort analysis--as variously illustrated in this
book--is used to probe the nature and degree of plasticity
(or constancy) in the aging process, and to specify the
conditions under which particular aspects of the aging
process are variable. In one respect, the comparative study
of cohort life-course patterns across historical time is
similar to comparing the life-course patterns of different
individuals or sub-groups of individuals within a single
cohort. More importantly, however, the method has the unique
advantage of affording a societal view of the full set of
co-existing cohorts, as they age together through time. Thus
cohort analysis opens the door to deeper understanding of the
systemic interdependence between changes in the lives of
individuals and changes in society, both past and future
(cf. Riley and Nelson, 1971).

Life-Course Transitions

The chapters in PART TWO by Foner and Kertzer and by
Winsborough focus on this dialectical relationship between
aging and social change, particularly as it centers in critical transitions in the aging process. Transitions, featured
also in each of the subsequent chapters of PART TWO, are those
turning points in the life course--such as entering school,
marrying, retiring--when individuals give up old roles and
take up new ones. In the conceptual model of the sociology
of age, each transition forms the nexus between the changing
life course of the individual and the changing age-stratified
society (cf. Eisenstadt, 1956; Riley, Foner, Hess, and Toby,
1969; Riley and Waring, 1976).

Anne Foner and David Kertzer analyze "Intrinsic and Extrinsic Sources of Change in Life Course Transitions" by comparing two widely differing types of societies: a sample of less well-developed societies in Africa, where age is a major and explicit element of social organization, and contemporary American society, where age is more loosely used as a criterion for role entry and exit. Foner and Kertzer find, contrary to long-held anthropological views, that life-course transitions are subject to change in both types of societies: because of problems intrinsic to transition processes and because of pressures from external events. Thus, on the one hand, societal rules of transition themselves give rise to conflicts and tensions, as each new cohort must contend with the older cohorts it is displacing, and these conflicts and tensions correspondingly press to change the norms and practices governing transitions. On the other hand, external forces--changes in fertility of the soil, changes in immunity, famine, pestilence, contact with other cultures, and other changes in the social and physical context in which transitions take place--also force alterations upon the existing transition procedures. Whether societies are marked by a slow or a rapid rate of social change, then, life-course transitions, and therefore the aging process, are rarely the same for successive cohorts.

Implicit in this argument is a provocative postulate: that the nature of the aging process is not merely changeable, as discussed in PART ONE of the symposium, but subject to a universal source of change: cohort flow. Because aging is continuous and inevitable, transitions over the life course have a rhythm that may appear inflexible: children become youths, youths are transformed into adults, and adults become old men and women. And yet this rhythm is continually disturbed by the immanent strains between societal requirements and individual needs, as the changing social structure must accommodate the perpetual flow of one cohort after another, and individuals must try to adapt to new roles and new intergenerational relationships. These strains on both individuals and society, which are intrinsic to the transition process itself, produce societal changes that, in turn, differentiate the life-course patterns of successive cohorts.

Halliman Winsborough, who also deals with changes in life-course transitions, is less concerned with the impact of these changes on the immanent tension between individual needs and societal requirements than with the processes underlying the changes. In his chapter on "Changes in the Transition to Adulthood," he provides empirical data on the timing of role transitions over several decades of United States history (see Winsborough, Figure 1). Comparing cohorts of males born

between 1911 and 1941, he shows that recent cohorts tend to
move more rapidly than their predecessors through the full
set of transitions from youth to adulthood:, completing
school, taking the first full-time job, entering and leaving
the Armed Forces, and embarking upon marriage. According
to other reports (e.g., Modell, Furstenberg, and Hershberg,
1976), these changes are part of a long-term trend: the
age of leaving the parental home, for example, has been
declining since the late 19th century, when most young men
remained at home into their early 20s. Clearly, the entire
life course of individuals living at particular periods of
history is affected by the timing of such critical transitions, as these transitions may tend to coincide, or may
follow one another in particular sequences.

Winsborough's main focus here is on the sequencing or
ordering of transitions. He asks whether the time at which
people decide to marry is governed by "norms of appropriate
age" for this transition or by "norms of ordering," so that
most men marry only after completing school. If transitions
are linked by norms of ordering, then a change in the age
distribution of an earlier transition may be simply reflected in the age distribution of a later transition. Examining the data, he indeed finds that a good deal of the shift
in the age at marriage from 1947 to 1971 reflects changes in
age of completion of schooling (changes that fluctuated
somewhat with the pressures of the peacetime draft). This
finding, apart from its general significance as an approach
to life-course analysis, is important because it re-directs
the search for historical explanation to focus on the earlier
education transition, rather than on the subsequent decision
to marry. Since the next step in the sequence is having
children, such an analysis throws new light on how it is
that cohorts vary so widely in size; in this instance, as
Winsborough suggests, military draft laws, by interfering
with completion of schooling, may have contributed to the
"baby boom" cohorts following World War II.

The Interplay Between
Aging and Social Change

The remaining chapters in the book--devoted respectively
to growing old, retiring, and dying--treat social change as
it relates not only to these transitions but to other aspects
of the life course as well. Like Winsborough, Peter
Uhlenberg uses cohort comparisons to examine social changes
in America. While Winsborough deals with changes in youthful
transitions, the focus of Uhlenberg's chapter is on "Demographic Change and Problems of the Aged." Uhlenberg's
approach is to look at old age by reconstructing full life-

course patterns of successive cohorts of old people, showing
how their earlier biographies relate to their later-life
characteristics and statuses. His chapter traces the cumulative impact of changes in major demographic variables (mortality, fertility, marital formation and dissolution, immigration, and urbanization) on the lives of cohorts born about
a generation apart (1870-74, 1900-04, and 1930-34). Describing marked cohort differences in their situation and
characteristics when they reach old age (around 1940, 1970,
and 2000 respectively), Uhlenberg discusses how secular
changes in later life stem from "the interaction of particular
cohort composition and the surrounding socio-demographic
environment." His projection of the most recent cohort into
the future is of special interest since it anticipates
Gordon's emphasis on futurism in the last chapter.

Uhlenberg also points to the reciprocal impact of these
cohort changes upon the society. As people's lives have
altered, the traditional social problems of old age, poverty,
and inadequate health care, have been substantially diminished, although a new and more subtle problem has been
emerging. There has been a widening gap between the abilities
of the older population (whose health, education, and financial status have been generally improving) and the decreasing
societal opportunities for the elderly to participate in
either the family or the labor force--a gap that may engender
new strains and the potential for still further change.

James Morgan also considers how the aging of different
cohorts may be understood in terms of their different historical experiences, as he addresses the question posed in
his chapter title, "What With Inflation and Unemployment,
Who Can Afford to Retire?" Morgan reports a recent small
re-assessment of people's retirement expectations which shows
an unexpected "kink" in the trend toward planning early
retirement: an older cohort that is now approaching retirement tends to anticipate early retirement (as it did ten
years ago), but the more recent, younger cohort appears <u>less</u>
favorable. How to account for the apparent change? Morgan
(though he complains of inadequate information) points to
facts that are known about the differing life histories of the
two cohorts. The earlier cohort (now aged 50-60) had a particularly favorable experience, entering the labor market at
the time of an economic upswing and achieving status, seniority,and job security before the unemployment of the 1970s.
By contrast, the subsequent cohort entered the labor market
in a less ebullient period, then they were obliged to compete
with the large numbers in the "baby boom" cohort and with the
entrance of many more women into the labor market, and when
government policies--more concerned with inflation than with

unemployment—may have lessened their chances for promotion
and security. Morgan refers also to a third cohort, still
too young to have been questioned about retirement plans,
who may be benefitting from the fact that "in this cohort,
people are scarce!" The small size of the cohort, giving
individuals less competition in getting good jobs, is coupled
with a pattern of marrying later, mostly marrying a partner
who also works, and having fewer children. Hence Morgan
speculates that this cohort, unlike its immediate predeces-
sor, may again be much better off and able to retire early.
Patterns of retirement, then, may tend to vary with cohort
size (cf. Waring, 1975).

Theodore Gordon carries into the future, where hard
research must be supplemented by "scenarios" and the views
of "experts," the discussion of consequences of changed
patterns of aging. In his chapter on "Prospects for Aging
in America," length of life becomes the crucial variable,
and Gordon draws attention to two types of current research
which may continue to influence the expected length of life
over the next several decades. The first aims to "square"
the survival curve, so that (as through disease control) more
and more people will live out their "normal" life span. The
second type of research aims to extend the life span of the
human species, by attacking directly the aging process itself. Gordon's scenarios challenge us to somber thought
about future consequences (in terms, e.g., of population
increase, changes in retirement age and in dependency ratios,
family considerations, health care costs). And his scenarios
ultimately challenge us to confront the meaning of death
from the perspective of the life course.

Some Policy Implications

As such studies as these explore the malleability of
the aging process, its responsiveness to social conditions
and social change, this new field of inquiry is inviting
attention from several sectors of public policy and professional practice: health, education, manpower development,
social welfare, law, the ministry, financial management,
mass communication (Riley, Riley, and Johnson, 1969). When
aging is viewed as a life-long process affecting individuals,
its plasticity signals the need for early prevention of ills
rather than post hoc therapy, for positive social contributions at every age. When aging is viewed as a collective
process affecting the entire society, its plasticity calls
for rational assessment of the impact of historical trends
and events, and considered anticipation of the future consequences of current changes and possible interventions
(e.g., Neugarten and Havighurst, 1977).

Thus, both Morgan and Winsborough properly warn of the dangers of deliberate change unless heed is given to the potential consequences. Morgan's caveat concerns the necessity of more information on pension rights, assets, and people's expectations about income and needs, before making any permanent alterations in the mandatory retirement age or the Social Security system. Winsborough counsels against legislative "tinkering" with early-life requirements for schooling, military training, or public welfare service, because of possible "strong, unintended demographic consequences which should be considered in relation to population as well as other social policy."

Suggested Changes

Although the symposium was not designed to emphasize remedial programs, most of the contributors see in the plasticity of the aging process the vision of a better life for people of all ages. Thus Cobb surmises that "the world would be a healthier place if training in supportive behavior were built into the routines of our homes and schools, and support worker roles were institutionalized." Uhlenberg, bemoaning the diminished role of older people in family and work, calls for societal changes to provide oncoming cohorts of the elderly new opportunities for responsibility and constructive activity. As one example, Uhlenberg suggests that the "younger old" (aged 65-69) might provide care for the "older old" (aged 70 and over). (In 1940 there were 1.4 "older old" persons for each of the "younger old"--a ratio that will have risen to 2.4 by the year 2000.) Baltes and Willis, directing their attention to the importance of socialization for optimizing the course of ontogenetic development, discuss the proposal that education be redistributed across the entire life course. They describe the current concentration of education in the early phases of life as congruent with traditional theories of development that stress childhood exclusively; then note the parallel implications of their life-span theories which assume plasticity and the potential for life-long development. The recommendation is, then, for educational interventions that allow multiple pathways for different individuals and subgroups, and that aim to prepare people for future changes both in their own lives and in the society. Gordon, encountering the probable increased competition for jobs resulting from survival of more people into old age, comes to complementary proposals for redistribution of work over the life course, via such new employment modes as sabbaticals, job sharing, or increased part-time employment.

Policy Planning and Cohort Comparison

In their emphasis on anticipating the future, these
ideas and caveats for policy on aging lead back to the
method of cohort comparison. Researchers and policy makers
who make use of this procedure have a special advantage: in
looking ahead, they can make use of what has already hap-
pened--what is already knowable--about the cohorts alive
today.

A few familiar examples[1]/will emphasize the principle.
Consider first the cohorts now in old age. We know that they
will soon live out their life span and die. As Uhlenberg
suggests, we also know that the "new" cohorts of old people
(those approaching 65) are not the same as the "old old"
(now 75 and over): the former are generally better educated,
have experienced greater affluence, are more positive about
their health, are more likely to be elderly women living
alone, etc. Thus in regard to policy, it is predictable
that the "new" old people will attach new meanings to their
last years and will shape them in new ways.

Similarly, we know a great deal about the cohorts now
in middle age. These cohorts will soon leave behind the
active nurturance of their children and not long after enter
the ranks of the retired. What sort of old people will they
make? We know that they came from the small Depression
cohorts, whose young women claimed the feminine mystique and
made motherhood a full-time occupation; whose young men made
the unusually swift transition into adulthood described by
Winsborough. We know that they are now experiencing a particularly acute "mid-life crisis"--pressured between two
sets of large cohorts: their parents and the baby boom that
they spawned. Such information can perhaps be useful in the
context of Morgan's questions, in assessing changes in mandatory retirement, for example, or in the age of eligibility
for Social Security. How will those cohorts, who now bear
the dependency burdens, react to possible changes in their
own security benefits once they become old?

Even for cohorts now in infancy, much is already known.
For example, they are the issue of the lowest birthrates
ever recorded in the United States. Presumably, in view of
advances in contraception, most were wanted children.
Greater longevity will mean a fuller complement of antecedent
kin. More will have pre-school educational experience. Will
they therefore be more secure than their predecessors?--

---

[1]/As developed by my colleague, Joan Waring.

healthier, brighter, more democratic? Or will their lives
be damaged by other current facts? To wit: more of today's
children are illegitimate than in the past, fewer--especially
among blacks--live with parents. Can anything be learned,
for example, through comparison with the Depression cohorts,
which were also small?

Many and important questions can thus be framed and
reasonable conjectures formulated through use of cohort
information. Thus studying the size and composition of
cohorts at one time--and making adjustments for selective
attrition or possible increase through migration--can help
in estimating requirements at another time. Or studying the
earlier life experiences of currently existing cohorts can
set the stage for more realistic scenarios of their possible
future lives. Cohort analysis is, then, a powerful tool,
not only for indexing past social change, but also in alert-
ing one to forthcoming change. It can be used to anticipate
and assess some of the possible consequences of social interventions. It is fundamental to intelligent policy development.

Although methodological and conceptual aids are emerging,
the full meaning of the life course perspective is not easy
to grasp. And once grasped, it is easy to lose. Yet the
chapters in this symposium bring us immeasurably closer to
an understanding of aging. Perhaps for the first time in
the history of this thorny topic, we are able to see sure
signs of cumulation, of the reach toward interdisciplinary
integration, of mutual efforts to formulate and specify a
common approach. Aging is viewed as life-long multi-faceted,
multi-directed. At the least, we can now predict that the oncoming cohorts we are examining will not age in precisely
the same ways as we who have preceded them. We are not
mired in any ineluctable process of aging.

References

Eisenstadt, S. N., 1956. From Generation to Generation:
  Age Groups and Social Structure. Glencoe, Ill.: Free
  Press.

Mannheim, Karl (1928), 1952. "The Problem of Generations."
  Essays on The Sociology of Knowledge, Paul Kecskemeti
  (ed. and trans.). London: Routledge and Kegan Paul,
  pp. 276-332.

Neugarten, Bernice L. and Robert J. Havighurst (eds.), 1977.
  Extending the Human Life Span: Social Policy and Social
  Ethics. Washington, D.C.: National Science Foundation.

Model, John, Frank F. Furstenberg, Jr., and Theodore Hershberg, 1976. "Social Change and Transitions to Adulthood in Historical Perspective." Journal of Family History, 1 (1), pp. 7-32.

Riley, Matilda White, 1976. "Age Strata in Social Systems," in Robert H. Binstock and Ethel Shanas (eds.), Handbook of Aging and the Social Sciences. New York: Van Nostrand Reinhold, pp. 189-217.

Riley, Matilda White, Anne Foner, Beth Hess, and Marcia L. Toby, 1969. "Socialization for the Middle and Later Years," in David A. Goslin (ed.), Handbook of Socialization Theory and Research. Chicago: Rand McNally, pp. 951-982.

Riley, Matilda White, Marilyn Johnson, Anne Foner, 1972. Aging and Society, III: A Sociology of Age Stratification. New York: Russell Sage Foundation.

Riley, Matilda White and Edward E. Nelson, 1971. "Research On Stability and Change in Social Systems," in Bernard Barber and Alex Inkeles (eds.), Stability and Social Change: A Volume in Honor of Talcott Parsons. Boston: Little, Brown, pp. 407-449.

Riley, Matilda White, John W. Riley, Jr., and Marilyn Johnson (eds.), 1969. Aging and Society, II: Aging and the Professions. New York: Russell Sage Foundation.

Riley, Matilda White and Joan Waring, 1976. "Age and Aging," in Robert K. Merton and Robert Nisbet (eds), Contemporary Social Problems (4th Edition). New York: Harcourt Brace Jovanovich, pp. 355-410.

Ryder, Norman B., 1965. "The Cohort as a Concept in the Study of Social Change." American Sociological Review (30), pp. 843-861.

Ryder, Norman B., 1972. "Notes on the Concept of a Population," in Matilda White Riley, Marilyn Johnson, and Anne Foner, Aging and Society, III: A Sociology of Age Stratification. New York: Russell Sage Foundation.

Sorokin, Pitirim A., 1941. Social and Cultural Dynamics, IV: Basic Problems, Principles, and Methods. New York: American Book Company.

Waring, Joan M., 1975. "Social Replenishment and Social Change," in Anne Foner (ed.), American Behavioral Scientist, 19 (2), pp. 237-256.

Intrinsic and Extrinsic Sources of Change in Life-Course Transitions

Anne Foner and David I. Kertzer

In all societies the aging process is punctuated by transition points--stages when individuals give up familiar roles and take on new ones. Because of the inevitability of aging, these transitions over the life course seem to have a universal rhythm: children become youths, youths are transformed into adults, and adults become old men and women. But we know that even in societies where the rate of social change is slow, the process of life course transitions and, therefore, the aging process are subject to change. In this chapter[1] we search for some universal sources of change in transitions by focusing on two contrasting types of societies, African age-set societies and contemporary American society.

We selected African age-set societies because they differ markedly from contemporary society in the United States. They are relatively small-scale, technologically undeveloped, and preliterate. Because they explicitly utilize age as a major element in their social organization, their age systems are particularly well-defined and are better documented than those found in most other preliterate populations. We base our analysis on 21 societies, those African age-set societies for which adequate documentation was available.[2]

Our findings challenge some long held views. The writings of Benedict (1938: 165-66) had suggested that there

---

[1] Portions of this chapter are drawn from a more detailed article (Foner and Kertzer, 1978; see references for full citation. © 1978 by The University of Chicago. [2] The 14 age-set systems, the seven generation-set systems, and the primary sources relied on for their documentation are listed in Appendix A.

would be smooth transitions in the African societies,
traumatic ones in our own society; constancy in transition
processes in the former case, and continual change in the
latter. Instead, in both types of societies, transitions
represent an inherent source of conflict in the society and
pose problems for the individual. It is responses to these
intrinsic problems of life course transitions that provide
one potential source of change in the very nature of transitions. Transitions are transformed also because of the
pressures of external forces, changes in the social and
physical environment in which transitions take place.

The Age Systems of Age-set Societies

Before discussing changes in transitions, first a few
words about the nature of age systems in age-set societies.
All societies have some form of age stratification; that is,
age is one basis for allocating social roles and important
societal divisions (Riley et al., 1972). Age-set societies
are distinctive in the extent to which their age systems are
formalized and the degree to which age provides a major basis
for role allocation. To understand the operation of these
age systems, it is necessary to make a distinction between
age grades and age sets.

Age grades are socially defined life stages (e.g., youth,
warrior, elder), each of which is associated with a set of
appropriate roles and with different social rewards. Age
grades thus constitute the strata of the age system. The
number of age grades in the societies under study varies from
as few as two to as many as eleven. In many age-set
societies, each successively older age grade is associated
with more highly rewarded roles. In a few, however, it is a
relatively younger age grade, such as the warriors, whose
members receive the highest social rewards. As we shall see,
differential rewards among age grades are at the root of
certain transition problems.

Age sets are named groups of people, usually males--full-
blown age-set systems for females are uncommon--who are of
similar age or generation and who are assigned joint membership in a named group. (Age sets are a special case of
cohorts, the more general term referring to people who enter
a social system at the same time and who age together.)
While these groups are commonly based on age similarity, in
seven of the African societies under study a generational
principle is also operative. Here a person's set membership
is partially or entirely determined by that of his father,
the individual belonging to the set which follows his father's
by a prescribed distance. Once a set is formed, whether

based on age or generation, it lasts the bulk of the life
course. Age-set members proceed together at prescribed
intervals of transition from one age grade to another.
These transitions are generally marked by public ceremonies.
Most people in age-set societies look forward to transition
to the next age grade because of the typically higher
rewards associated with successive grades. Passage to the
final grade, however, is frequently accompanied by loss of
power and prestige, something analogous to retirement in our
society.

Despite the fact that life course transitions in age-set
societies are organized and ritualized, these transitions are
neither simple nor smooth. They give rise to problems which
seem to be intrinsic to transition processes and which are at
the root of changes in transitions.

The Rules of Transition

One set of problems characterizing transition processes
in age-set societies stems from the transition rules themselves. For one thing, rules are not always precisely
defined. According to an abstract model, transitions in
age-set societies occur at fixed points--say every X years.
In most cases, however, the timing of transitions is uncertain because it is a product of deliberation rather than
of simple chronological determination. Further, the decision
to initiate a group of young men into an age set or to
authorize the transition from the first to the second grade
is never entrusted to the individuals making the transition.
In 19 of the 21 societies under study, this is the prerogative of the elders. In two societies it is the prerogative
of a younger age set which has the greatest political power
in the society.

Given that (1) the exact timing of transitions is often
uncertain, (2) those most concerned have least to do with
determining the time of transition, and (3) there are in-
equalities in power and prestige among age grades, "setting
the date" frequently leads to conflicts. Age sets which
stand to lose prestige and power through the transition often
try to delay the ceremonies; for example, their members may
beat up those who would replace them. Those who stand to
gain exert pressure to expedite the rites; they may be
disobedient or attack the role incumbents they wish to replace (Peristiany 1939:31-32). Since the ensuing struggles
concern all the men in several age sets, these conflicts
have a potentially great impact on the whole society. Of the
ten societies in our sample for which there are sufficient
data, all having indeterminate timing are reported to have

conflicts over the timing of transitions. The only society
having determinate timing of transitions, the Nandi, is the
only one for which the author specifically claims that the
transitions engender no social conflict (Huntingford 1953:
68).

Another set of problems arises in age-set societies
because certain rules of transition are too rigid. In these
situations the rules often lead to age discrepancies: there
is a wide gap in the ages of members making transitions
together or, alternatively, individuals of about the same age
are not permitted to make transitions together. For example,
among the Galla of Ethiopia, a generation-set society, many
children "retire" alongside elderly men who also belong to
the same generation set. Some men may not marry and have
children until they are in their forties, while others in
their generation set may do so in their twenties (Legesse
1973). Such problems are mentioned in reports of all seven
of the generation-set societies under study. In several age-
set societies having no generational component age discrepancies occur too, but primarily because initiation into an
age set depends not so much on chronological age but on
social maturity or family wealth (where initiation requires
a substantial offering). Once the recruitment of the age-
set membership is completed, however, subsequent role transfers are formally made by all age-set members together. For
example, if individual A was one of the oldest recruits to
the age set and individual B one of the youngest, the rules
would require both to "retire" at the same time, but A might
be 48 and B just 38 at retirement. The general point here
is that strict adherence to the rules of the age system can
have adverse consequences: needs of some individuals are
disregarded, as among those whose marriages are delayed or
whose retirement is forced prematurely; other societal norms
for what is age-appropriate behavior are violated; or
societal requirements for qualified personnel, such as
warriors of fighting age, are not satisfied.

In brief, we find a paradoxical situation. On the one
hand, because there are no clear rules mandating a specific
point at which transitions are to be made, conflicts tend
to arise between those who wish to assume age-graded roles
of power and prestige and those who are reluctant to be
kicked upstairs. On the other hand, explicit rules of life
course transitions can also create problems for the society
by subverting requirements for an adequate number of role
players of a given age or by creating frustrations which,
in turn, motivate some individuals to engage in anti-social
behavior.

Although age norms in our society may not stand out so clearly as they do in age-set societies, there are under-lying similarities. Age is one basis of allocation to im-portant roles; we recognize several broadly-defined age strata--for example, childhood, youth, middle age, and old age; and transitions from one age stratum to the next typically involve changes in roles and in rewards for role performance.[1] Some of the same problems stemming from both indeterminate and explicit rules of transition occur here as well and have far-reaching consequences for the whole society.

Consider, on the one hand, the indeterminancy of the timing of transitions. In our society, the assumption of full adult status, with all the privileges this entails, depends a good deal on having full-time work among males and increasingly among females. Yet unemployment rates are higher for younger than for older workers, especially at times of economic sluggishness. When full-time jobs are not available, the transition of young people to effective adult-hood becomes problematic. The uncertainty about when they will assume full adult status can be a source of youthful deviance and hostility toward people older than they.

On the other hand, the operation of explicit rules of transition also leads to problems in our society because such rules are not necessarily geared to the individual's readiness either to assume or to leave given roles. Further, because these clearly-defined rules affect a con-siderable number of individuals in an age stratum, the potential difficulties for the society are magnified. Manda-tory retirement, for example, has created dissatisfaction among many older workers. In the past, such enforced role ousters have led to various types of social withdrawal among older persons, an outcome creating problems for the family and the community. More recently, mandatory retirement has become an issue which pits interest groups of older people against those of younger adults.

Role Discontinuities

Another type of problem inherent in transitions, role discontinuities, also has implications for change in transi-tions. Discontinuities involve the content of roles, the

---

[1]For a fuller discussion of the nature of the age stratifica-tion system and the processes of aging and succession of cohorts in the United States, see Riley, Johnson, and Foner (1972); Riley (1976); Riley and Waring (1976); Foner (1975).

marked contrast between pre-and post-transition role definitions, as well as problems of pacing such as the abruptness
with which transfers are made. We are familiar with such
sharp changes in the person's roles at the time of transition
in contemporary American society--as in the transition from
adolescent to adult or from worker to retiree. Discontinuities occur also in many age-set societies. A dramatic change
often found in age-set societies occurs when boys are
initiated into an age set and occupy the first grade of an
age-set cycle; they move abruptly from the roles of children
to those of adults. For example, among the Tiriki (Sangree
1966), uninitiated boys may not engage in sexual intercourse;
they must eat with other children and with women; and they
may play freely in the women's section of the hut. After
initiation, they may engage in sexual intercourse, they are
expected to eat with other men, and they are forbidden from
entering the women's section of the hut. They are thus
abruptly cut off from the sphere of women and children and
catapulted into the company of adult men. To be sure, not
all transitions are characterized by such sudden changes.
Sharp role discontinuities at the onset of old age are
reported for only two of the age-set societies we studied.
Further, role discontinuities seem more acute in our own
society than in many age-set societies. Discontinuities
between pre-and post-transition roles in our society involve
not only sharp changes in role definitions but also in
physical settings, role partners, and role relationships.

Transition Problems:
Intrinsic Sources of Change

We have focused on various transition problems not only
for their inherent interest but also because they frequently
precipitate changes in transitions. Changes may be almost
imperceptible or they may be marked; they may involve just
one or two features of transitions or many--such as matters
of timing, formality of transitions, extent of role discontinuities, whether transitions are made on a group or
individual basis, and whether they involve many roles. Consider, first, the open or hidden struggles between the "ins"
and the "outs" over the timing of transitions. One outcome
of actual or threatened conflicts or of widespread deviance
may be a change in the transition process, For example, the
lowering of the voting age to 18 in the United States was a
result in part, at least, of the youth-adult conflict of the
1960's.

Second, where rigid adherence to societal rules might
have adverse consequences for the society, adaptations may
emerge which, in effect, change the rules. For example, in

one generation-set society, the Gabra of Kenya and Ethiopia
(Torry forthcoming), a boy is assigned at birth to the generation set three removed from that of his father. As the
rules call for a new set to be formed every eight years, the
boy should assume the roles occupied by his father at a 24-
year distance. But what if an older man has a son, let us
say, who is 44 years younger than he? This son, as all his
sons, will belong to a generation set three removed from his
own. As a result, the roles which the father only gained
access to at, let us say, age 40, the youngest son would
enter at age 20. Where the father reaches the grade of retirement at age 60, his son must retire at age 40. Since it
is possible that this younger son may himself have a son born
when he is 44 years old, the outcome of these rules could be
even more striking. Before long, a large number of children
would be born already retired! Actually, such an outcome has
not materialized because the rule to have a transition rite
every eight years is systematically broken--people attribut-
ing the transition delays to such factors as poor climate or
warfare. Whatever the stated reasons, these long postpone-
ments permit an age system to continue whose rigid rules of
transition would otherwise lead to societal and individual
disaster.

Third, problems of role discontinuities are also often
offset by flexibility in actual transition practices. Such
attempts to cope with problems of role discontinuities--
whether self-conscious or not--may indirectly result in
changes in the nature of the transitions. There is often a
period of role rehearsal which permits individuals to learn
new roles before they are official incumbents; in age-set
societies, men of junior age grade status may be allowed to
attend and take part in the elders' meetings; in our society,
young people learn about work roles in their part-time and
summer jobs and about marital roles through dating or living
together. Sometimes the role changes are made by stages,
thereby easing the abruptness of a role transfer--as in the
case of gradual retirement. To the extent that such flexible
practices are institutionalized, transition processes themselves are transformed. Perhaps such a process is taking
place in the transition to retirement in the United States
today. For example, among a national sample of men and women
aged 58 to 63 in 1969 16 percent of the men and 24 percent of
the women who had worked full time in 1969 shifted to
part time work by 1973 (Bond 1976). If substantial numbers
of older workers continue to shift from full-time work to
part-time positions, a form of gradual retirement will, in
effect, be established as one mode of easing the transition
to retirement.

It should be noted that flexible transition practices do not resolve all transition problems. For example, there are some age-set societies with both flexible practices and conflict over the timing of transitions. Flexible practices help the person to fit into new roles; they also help deflect tensions in the society by reducing individual frustration which might otherwise be expressed in deviant acts or directed against other age groups. But they do not guarantee that people will be assigned or permitted to keep highly rewarding roles. As long as there are a limited number of very desirable roles to be allocated among people of different ages, the potential exists for age conflicts over these roles. And as long as such age tensions are present, transition processes are subject to change.

In sum, whether problems which are inherent in transition processes lead to social conflict or engender flexibility in the age system, attempts to deal with the problems are likely to transform the nature of transitions. Let us now turn to pressures for change created by the different environments in which transitions take place.

Extrinsic Sources of Change
in Transitions

No matter how unchanging a society may seem to be, the context in which transitions occur continually changes and such changes are likely to produce changes in the transition processes themselves. In our society, for example, successive cohorts making the transition to adulthood have been affected by depression, war, civil rights struggles and the like. In age-set societies successive age sets differ in exposure to natural disasters and in contact with other societal groups; they have been affected differently by policies of colonial powers, the presence of religious missionaries, and by economic and political transformations. Such extrinsic changes often beget changes in transitions.

Consider the consequences of some of the momentous events that have "hit" age-set societies. Contact with western societies has led in some cases to atrophy of the age-set system. For example, the Zanaki generation class system declined and lost its political significance because it could not coexist with an effective German or British administration (Bischofberger 1972:72; see also Evans-Pritchard 1940: 260). Among the Nigerian Afikpo Ibo a similar, if more gradual, process also seems to have occurred. With many young men away at work or at school, it is now difficult to organize into an effective group and collect the funds necessary for an initiation, even under pressure from

the elders. And among the Bamileke of Cameroon, the formation of new age sets has been made more difficult by the
introduction of compulsory education, which takes the youths
away from home (Hurault 1971: 315).

Sometimes, with growing political complexity in the
larger society, elders lose power and prestige. For example,
Sidamo elders, who once had a monopoly on power, must now
compete with the Ethiopian court system (Hamer 1970).
Among the Afikpo Ibo, elders with their localized and traditional orientations are no longer effective political leaders
in a situation of increasing governmental complexity. Among
the Sidamo, youths have become less deferential toward the
elders; among the Ibo, there is now greater friction between
youths and elders over the locus of authority. Presumably,
now that the elder age grade no longer is associated with
great power, in both societies there is less incentive to
make the transition to this grade.

The abolition of warfare by the colonial powers has also
had a considerable impact on transition rites in a number of
age-set societies; for in many of them the age-set structure
provided the organizational framework for military operations.
Among the Tharaka of Kenya, for example, entry in an age set
occurred in adolescence and was marked by a circumcision
ritual (Lowenthal 1974). Upon joining the age set, youths
were placed in the warrior grade, responsible for the protection of the land and raiding activities. Once this military
activity was eliminated by outside forces, there was little
pressure on the boy to await physical maturity before
entering an age set. The result has been a progressively
declining age of transition into age-set membership.

These various social forces not only have a special
impact on a given cohort, but the reactions of the first
cohort to encounter new events are a legacy to those who
follow. In the United States, the early cohorts to confront
retirement as a mass phenomenon experienced sharp discontinuities in this transition and had few societal facilities
available. More recent cohorts now have role models--both
positive and negative--and in the society measures have been
taken which provide societal support for retirees, from
leisure programs to adult education to retirement villages.
Indeed, today many older workers seem to look forward to
retirement (e.g., Bixby 1976; see also, Barfield and Morgan
1970).

Parallels are found also in age-set societies. Among
the Afikpo Ibo, for example, initiation into an age set and
consequent recognition of adult status takes place when a man

is in his 30s. It used to be that if a man was away from
his village at the time his age mates were joining an age set,
he would be unable to join that age set, later joining a more
junior one instead, that which was open to recruitment when
he returned. In recent years, however, there have been so
many young men absent from their village for years at a time
that the norm has been changed, allowing men to join an age
set in absentia. Once the first group made the transition to
this way, an alternative transition mode became available to
subsequent cohorts.

The external environment affects transitions in still
another way, through its impact on the size of cohorts.
Abrahams (forthcoming) suggests, for example, that among the
Labwor of Uganda a numerically depleted senior age set may
encourage an older member of the adjacent junior age set to
give up his age-set affiliation and join the more senior set,
thus making the transition as an individual. Among the
Karimojong, the senior age set which makes the decision to
hold a transition may delay doing so until its numbers are
reduced by death or illness. It is at this point that the
uninitiated adults are emboldened to make public protests
and succession is seen as unopposable. Thus any events, such
as an epidemic or a natural disaster, that affect the relative sizes of the age set in power and that seeking power
will influence the timing of transitions and the relations
among age sets. In our society, too, transition points are
pushed up or pushed back to adjust to successive cohorts
of different size. The transition of especially large
youth cohorts may be delayed because there are not enough
jobs for them. The transition of a small middle-aged cohort
to retirement may be delayed in order to maintain the level
of experienced workers in the labor force (Waring 1975).

It should be noted that the size of a cohort may itself
be affected by the rules of transition. In more than one
age-set society rules sharply limited the period in which a
man was permitted to sire offspring. Among the Borana Galla
of Ethiopia, for example, Legesse (1973: 128) has suggested
that at one time men could only father children during an
eight-year period of the age cycle. As obedience to this
prescription resulted in population decline, the age norm
itself was changed. Similarly, among the Rendille of Kenya,
marriage and childbirth were limited by restrictive age-set
norms. Daughters of the men in every third age set had to
delay their marriages until their brothers married--some
women, therefore not being permitted to marry until they
were 35 or older. The Rendille maintain that in the past
such delayed marriage affected two of every three age sets.
According to Spencer (1973: 35), the custom led to a dwindling

population and resulted eventually in the abandonment of restrictions for one of the two affected age-set lines.

As these various examples suggest, size of a cohort may be affected by forces both external and intrinsic to transition processes but size, in turn, exercises an independent influence on transitions.

Conclusion

In our concluding remarks we shall suggest some broad implications of our findings for the analysis of age and aging.

First, we want to elaborate on the notion of immanent sources of conflict in the process of life course transitions. Because aging is continuous and inevitable, the society must accommodate the perpetual flow of one cohort (or age set) after another to fit into the available array of social roles. One solution is to allow "natural" forces to operate: younger people assume adult roles when they are ready to do so; older people give up roles when they are ready or when they die or become ill. Another solution is to regulate this continuous stream of people by establishing firm age norms for entering and leaving roles: that is, establishing clearly-defined points of life course transition. Both solutions are problematic and can have adverse consequences for the society: the first, because there is no guarantee that the readiness of those who must give up roles fits in with the readiness of those waiting in the wings; the second, because the age norms may not be in accord with the individual needs or societal requirements.

These problems parallel two forms of the pathological division of labor which Durkheim (1964) proposed as causes of class conflicts. On the one hand, there is insufficient regulation in that there are no clear norms for the timing of transitions—the anomic case. On the other hand, there _are_ clear rules, but they are not in accord with individual capacities, as in the extrusion of the healthy old from the labor force in our society, or the long delay in marriage in some age-set societies—the analogue of Durkheim's forced division of labor. But whereas Durkheim saw these pathological forms as temporary aberrations, we suggest that in the case of age stratification, age conflicts are intrinsic to transitions and that these conflicts are likely to be a source of change in age systems. Thus we propose a synthesis of two contrasting theories of class as they apply to age: Durkheim's approach points to _causes_ of age conflicts, while it is Marx, with his emphasis on conflict as a source of change, who suggests the _consequences_ of such conflict.

Our second point is that successive cohorts are not only acted on by external forces; they are also actors, instruments of continual change in transitions and, therefore, in the aging process. Each cohort facing a given transition does so in a unique historical context and deals with the problems of this transition in its own way. Successive cohorts thus reflect broad social and economic trends and, as they react to these trends, they are agencies of change. Cohorts are also bearers of change resulting from social conflict or adaptations to transition difficulties. As conflicts over transitions are resolved or as members of a given cohort fashion measures to deal with transition difficulties, the transitions are modified. Later cohorts making these transitions face a situation on which earlier cohorts have left their mark.

In sum, our brief comparison of transitions in vastly different societies suggests that there may be certain universal forces for change in transition processes. These stem both from structural properties of age systems themselves, what we have referred to as intrinsic sources of change, and from alterations in the social, political, demographic and physical environment, that is, extrinsic sources of change. Transition processes thus change as individuals and societies deal with the exigencies of the transitions themselves, and as they try to adapt to new environmental circumstances.

Appendix A

The age-set societies and the primary sources used for their documentation are: Afikpo Ibo (Ottenberg 1971); Arusha (Gulliver 1963); Kikuyu (Kenyatta 1938; Lambert 1956; Middleton 1953; Prins /1953/ 1970); Kipsigis (Peristiany 1939; Prins /1953/ 1970); Latuka (Seligman and Seligman 1925; 1932; Kertzer and Madison, n.d.); Masai (Jacobs 1958; Bernardi 1955; Fosbrooke 1948); Meru (Holding 1942; Lambert 1947); Nandi (Huntingford 1953); Nuer (Evans-Pritchard 1936; 1940); Nyakyusa (Wilson 1949; 1963); Rendille (Spencer 1973); Samburu (Spencer 1965; 1973); Tiriki (Sangree 1965; 1966); and Turkana (Gulliver 1958). The seven generation-set systems are: Borana Galla (Legesse 1973; Prins /1953/ 1970); Jie (Gulliver 1953); Karimojong (Dyson-Hudson 1963; 1966); Konso (Hallpike 1972); Kuria (Ruel 1958); So (Laughlin and Laughlin 1974); and Zanaki (Bischofberger 1972). Occasional reference is also made to societies outside of this sample, where adequate ethnographic reports were not published until after our original sample was drawn.

References

Abrahams, R. G. forthcoming. "Aspects of Labwor Age and Generation Grouping and Related Systems." In Age, Generation and Time: Some Features of East African Age Organization, edited by P. T. W. Baxter and Uri Almagor. London: Hurst.

Barfield, Richard E. and James N. Morgan. 1970. Early Retirement: The Decision and the Experience and a Second Look. Ann Arbor, Mich.: Institute for Social Research.

Benedict, Ruth. 1938. "Continuities and Discontinuities in Cultural Conditioning." Psychiatry 1 (May): 161-167.

Bernardi, Bernardo. 1955. "The Age System of the Masai." Annali Lateranesi 18: 257-318.

Bischofberger, Otto. 1972. The Generation Classes of the Zanaki (Tanzania). Studia Ethnographica Friburgensia, vol. 1 Fribourg: University Press.

Bixby, Lenore E. 1976. "Retirement Patterns in the United States: Research and Policy Interaction." Social Security Bulletin 39 (August): 3-19.

Bond, Kathleen. 1976. "Retirement History Study's First Four Years: Work, Health, and Living Arrangements." Social Security Bulletin 39 (December): 1-14.

Durkheim, Emile. 1964. The Division of Labor. New York: Free Press.

Dyson-Hudson, Neville. 1963. "The Karimojong Age System." Ethnology 2 (3): 353-401.

_____. 1966. Karimojong Politics. London: Oxford University Press.

Evans-Pritchard, E. E. 1936. "The Nuer: Age Sets." Sudan Notes and Records 29 (2): 233-269.

_____. 1940. The Nuer. Oxford: Oxford University Press.

Foner, Anne. 1975. "Age in Society: Structure and Change." American Behavioral Scientist 19 (November/December): 144-168.

Foner, Anne and David I. Kertzer. 1978. "Transitions Over the Life Course: Lessons from Age-Set Societies." Ameri-can Journal of Sociology, Vol. 83, (March): 1081-1104.

Fosbrooke, H. A. 1948. "An Administrative Survey of the Masai Social System." Tanganyika Notes and Records 26: 1-50.

Gulliver, P. H. 1953. "The Age Set Organization of the Jie Tribe." Journal of the Royal Anthropological Institute 83: 147-168.

_____. 1958. "The Turkana Age Organization." American Anthropologist 60 (5): 900-922.

_____. 1963. Social Control in an African Society. London: Routledge and Kegan Paul.

Hallpike, C. R. 1972. The Konso of Ethiopia: A Study of the Values of a Cushitic People. Oxford: Clarendon.

Hamer, John H. 1970. "Sidamo Generational Class Cycles: A Political Gerontocracy." Africa 40 (1): 50-70.

Holding, E. M. 1942. "Some Preliminary Notes on Meru Age-Grades." Man 42 (31): 58-65.

Huntingford, G. W. B. 1953. The Nandi of Kenya. London: Routledge & Kegan Paul.

Hurault, Jean. 1971. "Les classes d'âge dans le systeme social des Bamiléké (Cameroun)." Pp. 308-319 in Classes et Associations d'âge en Afrique dell'Ouest, edited by Denise Paulme. Paris: Plon.

Jacobs, Alan H. 1958. "Masai Age-Groups and Some Functional Tasks." Paper read at Conference held at the East African Institute of Social Research, Makerere College, Kampala, Uganda.

Kenyatta, Jomo. 1938. Facing Mount Kenya: The Tribal Life of the Gikuyu. London: Secker & Warburg.

Kertzer, David I. and Oker B. B. Madison. n.d. "The Latuka Age-Set System." Unpublished manuscript.

Lambert, H. E. 1947. "The Use of Indigenous Authorities in Tribal Administration: Studies of the Meru of Kenya Colony." Communication no. 16, School of African Studies, University of Capetown.

_____. 1956. Kikuyu Social and Political Institu-
tions. London: Oxford University Press.

Laughlin, Charles D., Jr., and Elizabeth R. Laughlin. 1974.
"Age Generations and Political Process in So." Africa 44
(3): 266-279.

Legesse, Asmarom. 1973. Gada. New York: Free Press.

Lowenthal, Richard A. 1974. Tharaka Age-Organization and
the Theory of Age-Set Systems. Ann Arbor: University
Microfilms.

Middleton, J. 1953. The Kikuyu and Kamba of Kenya. London:
Routledge & Sons.

Ottenberg, Simon. 1971. Leadership and Authority in an
African Society: The Afikpo Village-Group. Seattle:
University of Washington Press.

Peristiany, J. G. 1939. The Social Institutions of the
Kipsigis. London: Routledge & Sons.

Prins, A. H. J. (1953) 1970. East African Age-Class Systems:
An Inquiry Into the Social Order of Galla, Kipsigis, and
Kikuyu. Westport, Conn.: Negro University Press.

Riley, Matilda White. 1976. "Age Strata in Social Systems."
Pp. 189-217 in Handbook of Aging and the Social Sciences,
edited by Robert H. Binstock, Ethel Shanas, and Associates.
New York: Van Nostrand.

Riley, Matilda White, Marilyn Johnson, and Anne Foner. 1972.
Aging and Society, Vol. 3, A Sociology of Age Stratification. New York: Russell Sage.

Riley, Matilda White and Joan Waring. 1976. "Age and Aging."
Pp. 355-413 in Contemporary Social Problems, edited by R. K.
Merton and R. Nisbet. New York: Harcourt, Brace, Jovano-
vich.

Ruel, J. J. 1958. "Kuria Generation Sets." Paper read at
Conference held at the East African Institute of Social
Research, Makerere College, Kampala, Uganda.

Sangree, Walter H. 1965. "The Bantu Tiriki of Western
Kenya." Pp. 41-80 in Peoples of Africa, edited by James L.
Gibbs, Jr. New York: Holt, Rinehart & Winston.

_____. 1966. Age, Prayer, and Politics in Tiriki, Kenya. New York: Oxford University Press.

Spencer, Paul. 1965. The Samburu: A Study of Gerontocracy in a Nomadic Tribe. Berkeley: University of California Press.

_____. 1973. Nomads in Alliance: Symbiosis and Growth Among the Rendille and Samburu of Kenya. London: Oxford University Press.

Torry, W. forthcoming. "Gabra Age Organization and Ecology." In Age, Generation and Time: Some Features of East African Age Organizations, edited by P. T. W. Baxter and Uri Almagor. London: Hurst.

Waring, Joan M. 1975. "Social Replenishment and Social Change: The Problem of Disordered Cohort Flow." American Behavioral Scientist 19 (November/December): 237-256.

Wilson, Monica. 1949. "Nyakyusa Age-Villages." Journal of the Royal Anthropological Institute 79: 21-25.

_____. (1941) 1963. Good Company: A Study of Nyakyusa Age-Villages. Boston: Beacon Press.

Changes in the
Transition to Adulthood

Halliman H. Winsborough

This chapter comes from a research project whose aim is to construct statistical histories of the life course of birth cohorts in the United States from around 1900 to the present.[1]

A previous paper from this project describes how cohorts of males move through the life course transitions which make up the progression from school boy to married adult (Winsborough, 1978). It shows that recent cohorts move through this progression much more rapidly than did earlier ones. This chapter will explain how a part of this reduction came about. It will show the implications of this explanation for understanding cross-sectional change in the age-at-first-marriage distribution for males. The chapter will conclude with the conjecture that a similar explanation may account for some portion of the post-War baby boom.

[1]This research is supported by Grant #SOC75-20409 from the National Science Foundation. The Center for Demography and Ecology, which is supported by Population Research Center Grant (5PO1-HD058760), provided computer services. Some of the data used here derived from the Occupational Changes in a Generation II Survey, which was supported by National Science Foundation Grant (GI-31604X). D. L. Featherman and R. M. Hauser, principal investigators of that grant, kindly provided access to those data. Discussions of the subject of this paper with R. M. Hauser, Seymour Spilerman, Ronald Rindfuss, Dennis Hogan, Neil Fligstein, and Steven Gortmaker have been most helpful. All errors of omission or commission are, of course, the sole responsibility of the author.

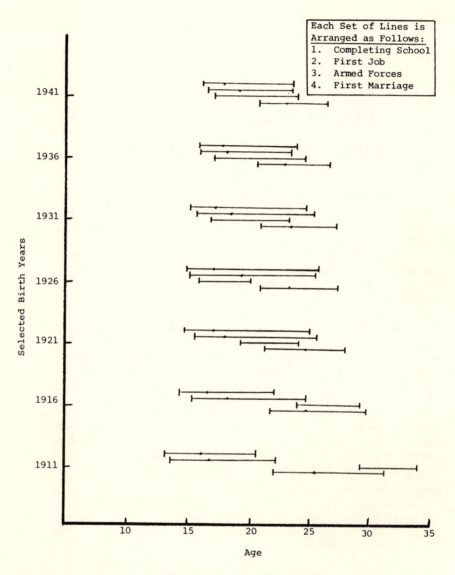

Figure 1.   Quartiles of the Age Distributions at School
Completion, First Job, Armed Forces Service and First Marriage
for Selected Birth Years.

Previous Findings

Transitions investigated in the previous paper as a part of the overall progression from school boy to adult were:
1. Completing school
2. Taking a first full-time job
3. Entrance to and exit from the Armed Forces
4. Entrance into first marriage.

The duration of each transition, i.e. the length of time it took a cohort to pass through the change, was measured as the difference in the respective ages at which twenty-five per cent and seventy-five per cent of the cohort had accomplished the passage. Figure 1 is a graph which shows these durations for selected cohorts. Data for this figure were computed from the Occupational Changes in a Generation II supplement to the March, 1973 CPS and from the 1970 Census tabulation of age at first marriage. In the figure, age is arrayed on the x-axis. Birth years are arrayed on the y-axis. The top line for each birth year indicates the duration of the school exit process. The line begins at the age when 25 per cent of the cohort had completed school, moves through the median age, indicated by a point, and terminates at the age at which 75 per cent of the cohort completed school. Similarly, the second line indicates the entrance-to-first-job duration; the third line, the duration of military service for those who ever served; and the fourth line, the duration of the first-marriage process. The main impression one gains from this figure is of the shortening of the progression as a whole. For the earliest cohorts the entire process took about 18 years. For recent cohorts it took slightly less than 10 years. Thus, the length of time a cohort spends in the transition from school boy to adult has nearly halved.

As the cohort transitions between major life course phases become shorter, the phases themselves must surely appear more distinct and more age associated. If, as preliminary evidence indicates, other transitions have also decreased in duration, then increasing segmentalization of life along the age continuum is an objective as well as a subjective social trend.

How has this decline in the duration of the transition to adulthood come about? A first step in proposing an explanation is to consider the kind of process under examination. A number of writers, such as Elder (1974), have suggested that the timing and perhaps the order of life course events are controlled by strong social norms. Hogan (1976) has recently shown that the majority of men move through the three transitions--school completion, labor force entrance, and marriage--in a typical order. Figure 2 reproduces Hogan's

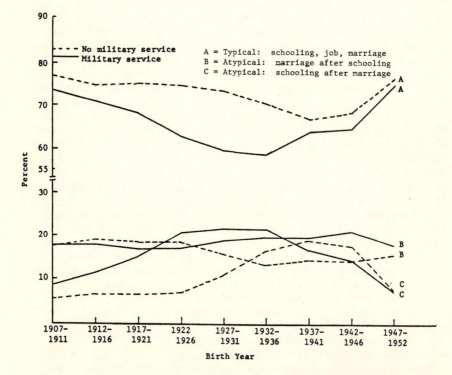

Figure 2.   Percent of Five-Year Birth Cohorts in Each of
             Three Temporal Ordering Categories by Military
             Service

graph of the per cent of five-year birth cohorts in each of
three categories of temporal ordering of events. Category A
represents the typical ordering of events--school, job,
marriage. Category B represents that ordering with one in-
version. Category C represents two inversions of the ordering. Figure 2 also shows whether or not the men have ever
served in the military. Although military service reduces
the proportions of men who show the typical ordering of
events, large fractions of veterans as well as non-veterans
do show the typical ordering. Hogan also investigates, <u>via</u>
a complex analysis, whether individuals seem to be responding
to norms of ordering or simply to norms of appropriate ages
for each transition. He concludes that order as well as
appropriate age is important.

Formal Aspects of an Explanation

The existence of a strongly adhered-to sequence of
events is important in thinking about how to explain changes
in duration of the progression to adulthood. If individual
transitions are "linked" by norms of ordering, then a change
in the distribution of an early transition will be "reflected
into" a change in a later one. Thus, if men usually marry
only after completing school and if, in the more recent
cohorts, fewer men prolong their school completion, then
fewer men will marry at a late age. Thus, over cohorts, a
"drawing towards the mean" of the right tail of the age-at-
school-completion distribution will also yield a "drawing in"
of the last quartile of the age-at-marriage distribution and
a consequent shortening of the overall progression to adulthood. All this can occur without a "behavioral" change in
the final transition--in how people decide to marry.

Although this principle is simple in concept, it is
more complex to detail how the first distribution in such a
sequential process "reflects into" the subsequent one. Consider a simple example. Suppose it were impossible to marry
until after school completion. Suppose there exists a probability of completing school in each year of age. Once
school is completed, suppose one is subject to a risk of
marrying specified by a given probability of first marrying
in each subsequent year. Under this arrangement, the chances
of marrying in any year of age is given by the sum of products
of these probabilities. The sum is over all younger ages.
For each younger age, the product is computed by multiplying
(1) the probability of completing school at that younger age
by (2) the probability of first marrying in the number of
years since school completion appropriate to the difference
between current age and the younger age. All of which is to
say that under the simple example, the age-at-marriage

distribution is a convolution of the age-at-school-completion
distribution and the years-after-school-completion first marriage distribution.

If the world were as simple as the example, that is, if
ordering rules always operated--if the behaviorally important
first marriage distribution depended only on time since school
completion and not upon age itself, and if the form of both
distributions could be specified--then there would be a
straightforward analytic solution to the influence of changes
in the prior distribution on the age distributions for the
subsequent events. Indeed, Coale and McNeil (1972) have
accomplished a decomposition of female first marriage rates
under the assumption that that distribution is a convolution
of a normally distributed probability of becoming marriageable
and a sequence of exponentially distributed waiting times for
such events as "keeping company," becoming engaged, and marrying.

The transitions investigated as a part of the passage
from school boy to adult do not seem to me to be amenable to
such elegant modeling, because norms of age as well as ordering appear to operate. Nonetheless, norms of ordering make
it reasonable to presume that some reflecting of changes in
school completion into marriage rates may be operating. If
such a reflection occurs, it is important for a substantive
explanation of changes in the overall progression. It means
that substantive explanations should first focus on why the
shift in the prior distribution occurred. It may be that a
large fraction of the "explanation" of change in the subsequent distribution is simply a reflection of those prior
changes.

In the following discussion I will argue that reflection
accounts for much of the change in the age-at-marriage distribution during the post-World War II period. The next
section will speculate about reasons for changes in the completion-of-education distribution. Then I will test the hypothesis that changes in the age-at-marriage distribution during
the post-war period are reflections of changes in educational
completion. All that follows will ignore entrance to the
labor force as part of the sequence of events--not because
that transition does not seem important but because of difficulties in the data[1] of relating the measure of timing for

---

[1]Data for this chapter are drawn from the 1973 Occupational
Changes in a Generation Supplement to the Current Population
Survey.

this event and the concept of first "real" labor force participation. This difficulty is one reason for here limiting
attention to the post-war eras. Surely the timing of labor
force entrance must have loomed large in explaining marriage
during the Depression.

Accounting for Changes in the Completion-of-Education Distribution: A Speculation

What can we say about changes in the age-at-school-completion distribution during the period between, say 1947 and
1971? During this time, the median number of years of education was rising. The age at which 25 per cent of cohort
members completed their education was also rising. The age
at which 75 per cent of cohort members finished their education, however, was falling consistently. The median duration
of the school completion process for the cohort of 1929 was
9.4 years. For the cohort of 1950 the median was 4.65 years.
The greater part of this decline is attributable to the shift
towards the median of the upper quartile of the distribution.

Why might such a change in the upper tail of the educa-
tion-completion distribution have occurred? Those were the
years of the peace-time draft. About half of the members of
birth cohorts moving to adulthood during that period served
in the Armed Forces. Although the necessity of service in
the Armed Forces undoubtedly disrupted the process of school
completion for many members of these cohorts, it may be that
the rules of the peace-time draft are in some measure responsible for the shift to younger ages of this upper quartile.
During most of the peace-time draft, deferments were available for men completing a normal block of schooling. Men in
college, for example, could retain deferred status as long
as they made "normal progress." A disruption of schooling,
however, resulted in a revocation of the student deferment
and, in many periods, a markedly increased chance of being
drafted. Because of this greater risk of being drafted,
students considering dropping out of school for a while found
it difficult to get good jobs, especially those which entailed
much on-the-job training. The draft laws, then, probably
generated incentives for students subject to the draft to
make normal and continuous progress through a recognized
regime of formal education. Thus it may be the effect of
these incentives on the progress of all draftable students
which skewed the completion-of-education distribution by
overwhelming the influence of disruption in completion due to
military service--disruption experienced by only a fraction
of those who actually served.

Table 1. Chi-square Statistics for a Backward Selection of Loglinear Models for a Table of Age by Nuptiality, by Period, by School Completion, by Military Status for Males 16-35 in 1947-1971.

Model # or Difference	Model of Description	Marginals Fitted	Degrees of Freedom	χ^2
(1)	All 4-way interactions	(MANS) (MANP) (MNSP) (ANSP)	1,368	816
(2)	Excludes (MANP) interaction	(MANS) (MNSP) (ANSP)	2,736	1,917
(2)-(1)	Tests exclusion of (MANP)		1,368	1,101
(3)	Reduces (MNSP) to (MNP)	(MANS) (MNP) (ANSP)	2,808	2,002
(3)-(2)	Tests reduction		72	85
(4)	Breaks up (ANSP) into (ASP) (ANP)	(MANS) (MNP) (ASP) (ANP)	3,264	2,502
(4)-(3)	Test division of (ANSP)		456	502
(5)	Drops (ANP)	(MANS) (MNP) (ASP)	3,720	3,040
(5)-(4)	Tests exclusion of (ANP)		456	535

M = Military Status
A = Age
N = Nuptiality
S = School Completion
P = Period

Source: OCG II Survey, March 1973.

I proceeded to undertake this analysis in the following
way. From the data, I made a table which classified men by
their age, military status, and school completion as of March
for each year from 1947 to 1971. I further classified men as
never-married or first-married in the subsequent year. Men
married in a previous year were dropped. Ages used were 16
to 35. Military status included: (1) not served to date,
(2) presently serving, (3) separated from service within the
year, and (4) service completed. The resulting table contained 8,000 cells representing 114,506 years of exposure to
the risk of first marriage.[1]

The resulting table was subjected to loglinear analysis
using a backwards selection technique for finding the optimum
model (Goodman, 1971).[2] The result of these procedures is
presented in Table 1.

The final model selected by this procedure (Model 4)
does include an age, period, nuptiality interaction. The
test of the null hypothesis that this interaction does not
exist yields a Chi-square value of 535 with 456 degrees of
freedom. The usual normal deviate approximation to probability levels for Chi-square distributions having large degrees
of freedom (i.e. $z = (2\chi^2)^{\frac{1}{2}} - (2v-1)^{\frac{1}{2}}$, where v is the degrees of freedom) yields a normal deviate of 2.53 which is
significant at about the .006 level. Thus, were there no
age, period, nuptiality interactions in the table, a Chi-
square value of this size would be unlikely by chance. Given
the large number of observations in the table, however, this
test is likely to be quite a powerful one. It is likely to
detect interactions which are substantively unimportant for
the purposes considered here. To investigate this possibility, I used the final model, excluding this interaction (i.e.
Model 5) to produce the expected age, period, nuptiality
table. I believe this process is analogous to a standardization procedure wherein the exposed population by age, period,
military status and school completion is applied to a set of
rates generated from the model.

Having produced the expected age, period, nuptiality
table, I proceeded to calculate age-specific rates for each

------

[1]Note that conditional odds of marrying computed from this
table are slightly biased upwards due to not including in the
never-married category fractional years of exposure for those
married in that year.

[2]For a demonstration that such a loglinear analysis is tanta-
mount to a logit analysis of the odds of marrying, see
Goodman, 1975.

Accounting for Change in the
Age-at-Marriage Distribution:
A Test of the Reflection Hypothesis

Whether or not this argument is a satisfactory explanation of the shift in the age-at-school-completion distribution, fairly marked changes did occur over this time period. What influence might these changes have had on the age-at-marriage distribution? By analogy to the simple model presented above we might expect them to be reflected in the subsequent distributions. From Hogan's work, however, we know that it would not be reasonable to presume that individuals, especially in this period, are subject to the risk of marriage only after completing their education. Rather, it is more reasonable to presume that the odds of marrying at each age change according to whether or not a man has completed his education and, perhaps, his military service. The problem, then, of testing the reflection hypothesis can be restated as seeing if the observed changes in age at marriage in successive cohorts can be generated by a model in which a set of conditional odds of marrying at particular ages is, in some sense, fixed over time. This logic is familiar to demographers as being similar to a complex "standardization" problem.

Rather than treating the problem as one requiring a direct standardization, however, I have chosen to generate a table from the data which can be thought of as containing the odds of marrying conditional on age, period (date), school completion, and military status. Using loglinear methods, I have tried to generate a model which "explains" the fluctuation in these odds. Such a model might assert that there was a separate schedule of odds of marrying by age for each military and school completion group. It might also hold that those age-specific odds are inflated or deflated by a constant amount in a given period. Such multipliers would simply adjust for changing volume of marriages without rearranging their distribution by age. Indeed, there might be separate inflation or deflation factors for period by military status by school completion and still not directly affect the age distribution of nuptiality odds. So long as there does not appear to be an interaction among age, nuptiality, and period, we can conclude that gross changes in the age-at-marriage distribution over time are a result of men moving through the separate age schedules of risk for school completion and military service as well as temporal shifts in the volume of marriage by categories other than age. It would not be necessary, then, to posit some exogenous, behavioral shift over time in age-at-marriage preferences.

period. Then, in synthetic cohort fashion, I calculated
the quartile levels of the age-at-marriage distribution for
a cohort of males living through the schedule for each
period. Figures 3, 4, and 5 compare these expected levels
with those computed from the observed table. The expected
levels match the main temporal shifts in age at marriage.
Expected distributions miss some of the lowering of the
age-at-first-quartile during the Korean War and somewhat
everestimate the median and third quartile age during the
late 1950s. Overall, however, this model excluding age,
period, nuptiality interaction tracks the changes in the
age-at-first marriage distributions fairly well.

Thus, it seems fair to assert that a good deal of the
shift in the age-at-marriage distribution for males from
1947 to 1971 is a reflection into this generally "subsequent"
distribution of changes in the cohort processes of completing
school and fulfilling their military "obligation."

Implications of these Results

Shifting from the cross-sectional to the cohort perspective, it is likely that a good deal of the change in
duration of the transition from school boy to adult occurring
for cohorts going through this transition in the post-war
period is a result of changes in the age-at-school-completion
transition and movement in and out of military service.
Earlier, I speculated that changes in school completion might
be accounted for by the existence of the post-war draft. If
that speculation is correct, we might perhaps predict some
significant post-1970 changes in the age-at-school-completion
distribution and consequent changes in age at marriage.

The next important life course steps for men subsequent
to first marriage are birth of first child, second child, and
so on. Since the presumed changes in the age distribution of
these events are certainly conditional upon age at marriage,
might they not also reflect the influence of changes in the
completion of schooling process and the process of military
service? It is not possible to answer this question directly
from the data of this study because no fertility information
is available. Indeed, precious few data of any kind are
presently available on male fertility--certainly not data
which jointly contain information on age at school completion,
age at initiation and termination of military service, age
at first marriage, and age at birth of first child. Given
this dearth of data and the expense of creating them, perhaps
a conjecture about what they might show is appropriate.

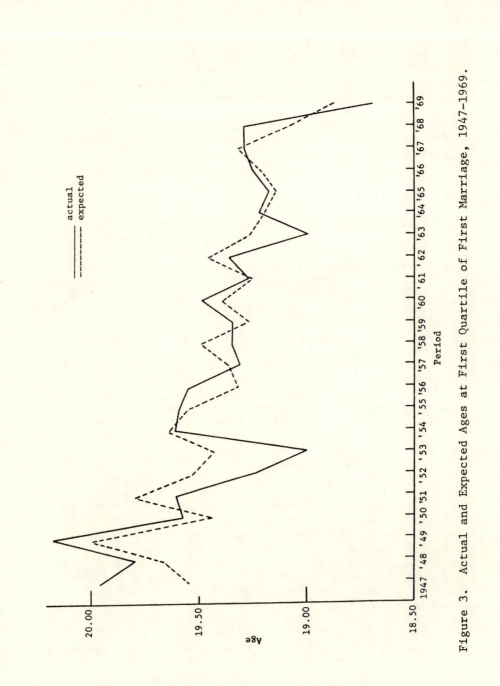

Figure 3. Actual and Expected Ages at First Quartile of First Marriage, 1947–1969.

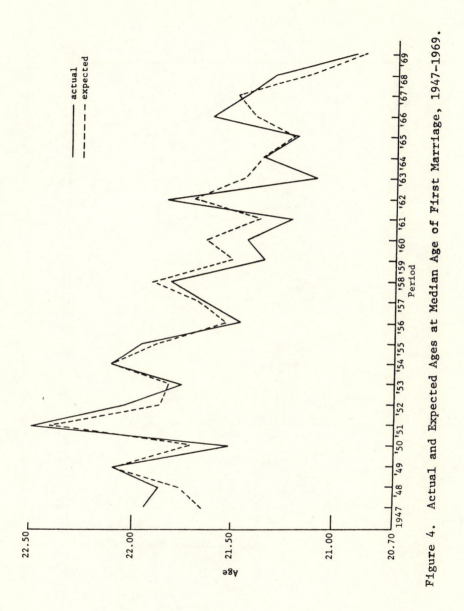

Figure 4. Actual and Expected Ages at Median Age of First Marriage, 1947-1969.

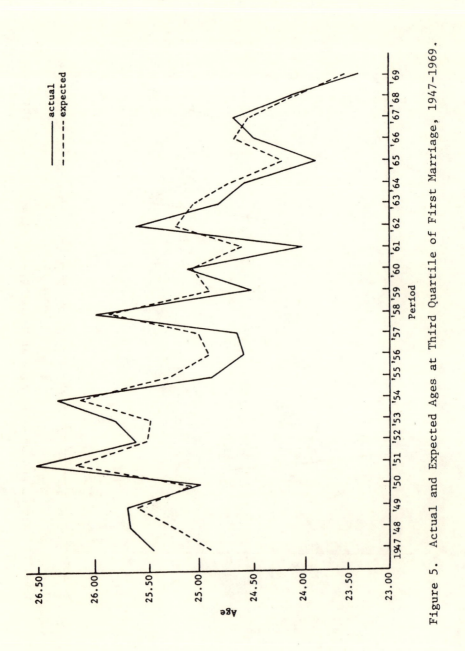

Figure 5. Actual and Expected Ages at Third Quartile of First Marriage, 1947-1969.

It seems to me possible that changes in the completion of schooling distribution and the intervention in the male life course of the "peace-time" draft may be important ingredients in explaining the post-World War II baby boom. It may be that the conditional odds of having a child by age for school completion, military status, first marriage, and such categories are relatively constant over time. It may be that the "social forces" moving the population through these transitions are the operative agent in generating the large number of births during the boom. That the existence of the peace-time draft plays an important role in this scenario does not offend conventional wisdom. We know that military call-ups play havoc with marriage and fertility schedules. Might not a more or less permanent emergency play a similar but more persistent role?

If there is any truth in this conjecture it would be important to know about. Discussions about reintroduction of the draft are presently under way. In general, the polity seems quite willing to "tinker" with aspects of the early life course through laws about the minimum amount of schooling required, the institution of peace-time drafts, proposals for universal military training, and even periods of general "public welfare" service for young people. Such policies may have strong, unintended demographic consequences which should be considered in relation to population as well as other social policy.

References

Coale, Ansley J. and D. B. McNeil
    1972   "The Distribution by Age of the Frequency of First Marriage in a Female Cohort." *Journal of the American Statistical Association*, Vol. 67, No. 340:743-749.

Elder, Glen
    1974   *Children of the Great Depression*. Chicago: The University of Chicago Press.

Goodman, Leo
    1971   "The Analysis of Multi-dimensional Contingency Tables: Stepwise and Direct Estimation Methods for Building Models for Multiple Classification." *Technometrics*, Vol. 13:33-61.

    1975   "The Relationship Between Modified and Usual Multiple Regression Approaches to the Analysis of Dichotomous Variables." In David Neiss (ed)., *Sociological Methodology*, pp. 83-110.

Hogan, Dennis P.
    1976   "The Passage of American Men from Family
                of Orientation to Family of Procreation:
                Patterns, Timing and Determinants." Ph.D.
                dissertation, Department of Sociology,
                University of Wisconsin-Madison.

Winsborough, Halliman H.
    1978   "Statistical Histories of the Life Cycle of
                Birth Cohorts: The Transition from School
                Boy to Adult Male." In Karl Taeuber (ed.),
                Social Demography: Research and Prospects.
                New York: Academic Press.

8

Demographic Change and Problems of the Aged

Peter Uhlenberg

Over the twentieth century two fundamental changes affecting the last stage of the life course, old age, have occurred. In a curious way, while those two changes have substantially diminished the importance of two basic social problems of old age, they have also created a new and far more subtle problem for the elderly in American society. An understanding of these changes and of the challenge they present for the future requires that we view contemporary old age in its historical context; that we look both at the past several decades and at the next ones.

Consider first how change in the composition and characteristics of the older population is responsible for altering the nature of old age in the United States. A continual process of change in the membership of the older population is going on. New cohorts of entrants cross the boundary which marks the beginning of old age while former members of the older population exit due to death. Since the new entrants differ from those exiting both in numbers and in characteristics, the character of the older population does not remain constant over time. Let me give two illustrations of this dynamic process in operation.

1. As a consequence of various historical demographic processes, approximately 1.7 million persons entered the population over age 65 in 1975, while only 1.2 million exited from this population. Thus the older population grew by .5 million persons. Those entering were born in 1910, were 35 years old at the end of World War II, and lived out most of their adult years during a period of rapid economic expansion.

Partial support for this study came from the Carolina Population Center.

The median number of years of school completed by the "new" old people was 10.5. The mean age of members of the older population who died in 1975 was 78, their median number of years of school completed was only 8.9, and an important decade of their adult lives was shaped by the Great Depression. The contrast between those entering and leaving the older population in this one year is striking.

2. The change in composition of the older population over the decade 1970-1980 is even more dramatic. During this decade there is a net change of about 4.5 million persons in the population over age 65, but this is the result of very large gross changes: about 17.5 million entrants and 13 million deaths to older persons. Thus a 63 per cent turnover in the composition of the older population is occurring in one decade, and this change in composition allows rapid changes in characteristics of the elderly.

I shall return to more carefully examine the actual extent of change and its implications, but now let us note the second (and closely related) change in the nature of old age.

In addition to a change in composition of members, the social structure of the old age stage of the life course has changed markedly. What are some structural changes that have affected the social, economic and political milieu within which cohorts of older persons live out the last stage of their lives? Societal role expectations for the elderly with respect to labor force participation and family responsibilities have changed. Organized groups concerned specifically with the needs of the elderly have rapidly expanded: 3 million persons are affiliated with the National Council of Senior Citizens, and more than 9 million are dues-paying members of the National Retired Teachers Association--American Association of Retired Persons (Pratt, 1976). Government intervention programs directed toward the needs of the elderly (Social Security, Medicare, nutrition programs, etc.) have developed and grown in scope and, with the ever growing number of gerontologists whose careers depend upon maintaining the salience of the needs of the elderly and upon proposing new solutions for them, we may anticipate continuing changes in the structure of old age.

Social problems affecting the aged at any particular time arise from the interaction of the existing characteristics of the aged and the existing social structure of the old age stage. The essential change in composition over this century is a dramatic increase in the proportions of the older population who are urban, native-born, well-educated, and financially secure. The structural changes have greatly increased resources available to the elderly--money, medical care, and recreational possibilities.

The combined effect of these changes is a tremendous reduction in the problems of poverty and inadequate health care for the aged--two big problems that have been notably ameliorated by changes over this century. The per cent of persons over age 65 classified as below poverty level by the Census Bureau dropped from 37.2 in 1959 to 15.7 in 1974. A very similar figure for 1974 came from responses of the elderly themselves in a Louis Harris survey (Harris and Associates, 1975): 15 percent of the elderly indicated that insufficient money to live on was a serious problem affecting them. From this same survey it was found that 21 per cent of the older population considered poor health a serious problem for themselves. Clearly problems of poverty and health care for the aged have not been eliminated: the proportions reported above correspond to 3.1 and 4.4 million older persons plagued with poverty and poor health respectively, and blacks are disproportionately represented in these categories. But compared to conditions in the past, the reduction in these problems is tremendous. And current trends indicate that continued reductions should be expected. First, the changing characteristics of the older population point to continued reductions. As indicated by the following table,from the Harris survey, problems of poverty and health are most severe for the poorly educated elderly--a category which is rapidly declining.

| | Education | | |
"Very serious" problem	Less than high school	High School-Some college	College 4 years or more
Poor Health	26%	14%	9%
Poverty	20%	8%	3%

Second, the direction of government policy with respect to an income floor and health insurance point to continued reduction of these problems. So changes in old age are seriously reducing the strength of the age-old problems of old age--poverty and inadequate health care.

But consider another consequence of the changing nature of old age. As already noted, the changing composition of the elderly population (improved education and health, more relevant experience for functioning in a complex society, etc.) is substantially increasing the capacity of this population to contribute to societal welfare. But an examination of the changing structure of old age reveals the increasing removal of responsibilities from the elderly. This is most clearly seen by removing the aged from responsibilities for economic productivity. Additionally, the diminished role of the elderly in families, the removal of the need to provide for self in a welfare state, and the exclusive emphasis upon leisure activities for the elderly all point to a social definition of old age as a period of reduced responsibility. The impact of these changes is a rapidly widening gap between the abilities of the older population, on the one hand, and the responsibilities and opportunities for the elderly to use their abilities constructively, on the other. It is inconceivable that old age is going to be a positive stage of the life course if it is devoid of purpose and fails to provide social roles in which constructive activity is expected. But this is the direction in which old age is moving. And this is the emerging problem of old age which deserves serious attention and creative action.

Now that I have revealed the thrust of my argument, let me return to more carefully develop the basis for discussing change in old age. The starting point is an understanding of the place of age strata in society, and of the current attention to the old age stratum.

Attention to Old Age

Age as a major basis for stratification of society has received considerable attention in recent years (Riley, Johnson, and Foner, 1972; Neugarten and Hagstead, 1976). While there is some arbitrariness in how age strata are defined, it is clear that norms regarding age-appropriate behavior exist, and that individuals are socialized so that they behave according to these norms (Neugarten et al., 1965). Sanctions, varying from laws to informal disapproval communicated by frowns, are employed to encourage conformance to behavior considered appropriate for a particular age stratum. The pervasive influence of age upon individuals is recognized by Riley (1976) when she writes:

A person's activities, his attitudes toward life, his relationships to his family or to his work, his biological capacities, and his physical fitness are all conditioned by his position in the age structure of the particular society in which he lives.

As an individual lives out his life course, he moves through a succession of age strata: infancy, childhood, adolescence, etc. And the individual moves through these stages as a member of a cohort which is aging through historical time. The experience of the cohort during a particular stage of the life course is determined by the social structure of that stage at that historical time, as well as by the unique composition of the cohort (determined by past events) and the unique historical environment existing at that time. Thus a complex, dynamic process goes on over time which constantly alters the nature of a society's age strata.

Attention to old age as a stage in the life course has been increasing for several reasons:

1.   Over this century the boundary line that defines entrance into old age has sharpened and old age has now clearly emerged as a distinct stage. Age at which retirement is expected or required, age at which social security benefits begin, and age at which special discounts begin (bus fares, entrance fees, prescription drugs, etc.) have all become standardized and mark the chronological age at which the last stage begins.
2.   Since 1900 the proportion of the total population over age 65 has increased by 2.5 times, and now 10 per cent of the population is in the old age stage. In absolute terms, the number of persons over age 65 in the U.S. is greater than the entire combined populations of Denmark, Finland, Norway, and Sweden.
3.   Since 1960 increasing attention and debate has been focused upon the role of government intervention in social problems, and problems of the elderly have been an important component of this. Special committees in the House and the Senate, the Administration on Aging, the National Institute on Aging, and court cases on legal aspects of age all reflect the increasing salience of old age as a national issue of major significance.
4.   The status of "old" is widely held in low esteem, and yet each person will be ascribed this status if he or she but lives the expected number of years.
5.   Finally, as an area of study within life-course research, old age is particularly interesting because at this stage the cumulative impact of a whole lifetime of experiences can be examined.

The surge of interest in aging and old age has stimulated much new scientific research in the field of gerontology. The prevailing stereotype of old age, which has been firmly

rooted and entirely unflattering, is being demolished as researchers empirically examine the reality of old age in American society. In fact, dispelling myths about old age has
been the overriding interest of gerontologists. So we now
know a great deal about the attitudes, behaviors, and social
conditions of the elderly. This information is invaluable
for efforts to enhance the quality of life for the elderly.

Nevertheless, concentration upon the reality of life for
the contemporary older population cannot offer a satisfactory
understanding of old age, because this ahistorical perspective fails to include the dynamic process that is altering
the nature of old age. The examination of old age in historical context is a pressing challenge for the social sciences.
This paper is a modest attempt to look at the process of
change by focusing upon the impact of demographic change.
Demographic change both alters the social milieu existing
when successive cohorts enter old age and it alters the characteristics of the successive cohorts entering old age.

Life Course Patterns of Three Cohorts

To see the direction of change in characteristics of
successive cohorts entering old age, I will look at the life
course experiences of three particular cohorts. The birth
period, and dates at which each cohort occupied selected age
categories, are given in the following table:

Birth Cohort	Born	5-9	15-19	35-59	65-69
				Age	
1870	1870-74	1880	1890	1910	1940
1900	1900-04	1910	1920	1940	1970
1930	1930-34	1940	1950	1970	2000

It is apparent that the 1900 cohort entered old age around
1970, while the 1870 cohort preceded it by about one generation and the 1930 cohort will follow it by about one generation. The change observed among these cohorts roughly indicates the amount of change in the older population over the
last half of the twentieth century.

Let us quickly move through the life course of each of
these cohorts, from childhood to old age, looking for the impact of demographic change. In each of the three tables,

reading across a row indicates the changes between generations, while reading down a column gives a picture of the
life course of a particular cohort.

   Childhood. The context of childhood (see Table 1) for
most members of the 1870 cohort was a large family in a rural
area. Over three-fourths lived in rural areas, and 80 per
cent had 4 or more siblings. For 86 per cent of these individuals, schooling ended before the completion of high school
and, by current standards, early entrance into the labor
force was the norm. Death within the family of orientation
was a common experience, with 27 per cent having one or both
of their parents die before they reached age 15. During this
time period the probability that all 5 children born into a
5-child family would survive to age 15 was less than .2.
Thus intimate contact with death during childhood was a nearly universal experience for members of this 1870 cohort.

   Decreasing mortality and fertility and rapid urbanization between 1870 and 1940 produced a very different childhood context for the 1930 cohort. About equal proportions
grew up in urban and in rural areas, and only about one-third
had as many as 4 siblings. Years of schooling were stretched
out, and death of parents or siblings became a relatively un-
common experience (due both to the vast reduction in death
rates and the reduction in family size). The effects upon
behavior in later life course stages of these changes in the
context of early socialization remain virtually unexplored,
but they almost certainly are not trivial.

   Adulthood. These three generations are as distinctly
differentiated in experiences of adulthood as they were in
childhood (see Table 2). The following fairly uniform changes occurred across the three cohorts at this life stage:

   1.   The pace of immigration declined, so that successive
        cohorts were decreasingly composed of foreign-born
        persons.
   2.   The continual movement away from farms steadily de-
        creased the proportion living in rural areas, so
        that nearly three-fourths of the most recent cohort
        spent their adult years in urban environments.
   3.   The changing occupational structure led to a marked
        decline in the proportion of males engaged in farm-
        ing and a corresponding increase in the proportion
        in white-collar jobs--particularly in professional
        positions.
   4.   The changing marital patterns produced a steady de-
        cline in proportion of women who remain spinsters
        throughout their adult lives, and has greatly in-

Table 1. A Demographic Perspective on the Childhood Characteristics of Three Cohorts.

Cohort Characteristics	Cohort of: 1870	1900	1930
Size when aged 5-9 (in '000s)	6480	9761	10684
% rural when 5-9	78%	59%	51%
% distribution by no. of siblings:			
0-1	6	14	29
2-3	14	25	34
4+	80	61	37
% with parent who died (before the (child reached age 15)	27	22	11
% distribution by no. of school years completed:			
less than 8	44	28	8
8-H.S. 3	42	45	25
H.S. 4+	14	27	67

Table 2. A Demographic Perspective on the Adulthood Characteristics of Three Cohorts.

Cohort Characteristics	Cohort of: 1870	1900	1930
Size when aged 25-29 (in '000s)	6529	9834	10804
% foreign-born when aged 25-29	17%	11%	3%
% rural when aged 25-29	47	37	28
% distribution of males by occupation when aged 35-39			
White-Collar	NA	31	44
Blue-Collar (non-farm)	NA	52	53
Farm	NA	17	3
Marital Status of females:			
% never married by age 50	10	8	5
% divorced by age 40-44 (of those ever-married)	NA	11	21
% distribution of females by children ever born:			
0	23	28	13
1-3	36	51	52
4+	41	21	35

creased the proportion who experience divorce.
Nevertheless, marital instability before old age has
not increased, because of the declining impact of
mortality during the middle years of life.

The childbearing experience of successive cohorts has not
changed uniformly, but the sharp decline in childlessness between the second and third cohorts should be noted. Far
fewer of the women entering old age in the coming years of
this century will be single or childless than has been the
pattern up to now.

   Old Age. To complete the demographic profile of these
three cohorts, let us look at their characteristics at the
time each is entering old age (see Table 3). The size of a
cohort at this stage differs from its initial size because of
two competing forces: the addition that occurs over the life
course due to net migration and the attrition that occurs due
to death. The impact of both of these demographic processes
has declined over time, as immigration has slowed and mortality prior to old age has dropped precipitously. The decline
in mortality has exerted the stronger influence, so that the
cohorts are more differentiated in size at old age than they
were at childhood. While at ages 5-9 the 1930 cohort was 1.5
times larger than the 1870 one, by ages 65-69 it will be 2.4
times larger.

   As a result of increasing sex differences in survival
rates, the sex ratio for cohorts entering old age has changed
from near equality to a situation where there are 10 females
for every 8 males. Further, as the cohorts move through old
age, they become increasingly dominated by females. The average number of years of life remaining for a female at age
65 is now 17.1, compared to 13.1 for males. As is well known,
the combination of female superiority in longevity combined
with the tendency for women to marry men older than themselves leads to the situation where the typical woman can anticipate living the last years of her life as a widow. For
males in old age, a movement of great significance has been
the institutionalization of retirement around age 65. Among
men in the 1870 cohort, 59 per cent were still in the labor
force when they were aged 65-69, but this declined to 39 per
cent for the 1900 cohort and is expected to drop below 25 per
cent for the 1930 cohort.

   In summary, demographic and social change since 1870 has
produced widely varied life course experiences for cohorts
born a generation apart, and has significantly altered the
nature of old age by changing the characteristics of the persons occupying this stage of life. Increasingly, cohorts

Table 3. A Demographic Perspective on the Old Age Character-
         istics of Three Cohorts.

| | Cohort of: | | |
Cohort Characteristics	1870	1900	1930
Size when aged 65-69 (in '000s)	3807	6992	9023
% of initial cohort surviving to age 65:			
Males	37%	50%	63%
Females	42	62	77
% foreign-born when aged 65-69	21	13	7
Sex ratio when aged 65-69	99	81	80
Average no. of yrs. of life remain-ing at age 65:			
Males	11.7	13.7	?
Females	12.8	17.1	?
% of males in labor force when aged 65-69	69	42	25
Ratio of age groups 70+/65-69, when aged 65-69	1.4	1.8	2.4

entering old age are composed of individuals who are native-born and who were reared in moderate-sized families in non-farm environments. They have completed at least 12 years of formal schooling and have been employed in jobs requiring participation in modern, complex organizations. Upon reaching age 65, an increasing majority can anticipate 15 or more remaining years of life with reasonably good health and without serious threat of poverty. For males, the last years of life will be in a state of retirement, and for females they will be in a state of widowhood. Given such circumstances, what are the most pressing problems of old age that need our attention?

Conclusions

In an article on successful aging, Robert Butler (1974) wrote the following insightful comments regarding the last stage of the life course:

> Old age is a period when there is a unique de-velopmental work to be accomplished. Childhood might be broadly defined as a period of gathering and enlarging strength and experience, whereas the major developmental task in old age is to clarify, deepen and find use for what one has already ob-tained in a lifetime of learning and adapting. The elderly must teach themselves to conserve their strength and resources when necessary and to adjust in the best sense to those changes and losses that occur as part of the aging experience. The ability of the elderly person to adapt and thrive is con-tingent upon his physical health, personality, earlier life experiences, and on the societal sup-ports he receives, i.e., adequate finances, shelter, medical care, social roles, and recreation.

While I agree with this entire statement, the thrust of this paper is particularly relevant to the last sentence—which specifies things which determine the ability of the elderly to succeed in old age. As dynamic processes change the na-ture of old age, the relative importance of these different factors will change. I would like to suggest four conclu-sions from this paper which bear on the issue of intervention to improve the ability of the elderly to age successfully.

1. The first contingencies noted by Butler are physical health, personality, and earlier life experiences. By the time a cohort enters into old age, these factors have been largely determined. Thus if intervention is to affect these, or other characteristics determined earlier in life, it must

occur at an earlier stage of the life course. A comprehensive view of old age must not focus only upon old age, but must view old age as the culmination of an entire life course. Intervention through the educational system in the early stages of life is one example of how future cohorts could be better prepared for old age. Similarly, policies resulting in improved health care or nutrition in earlier life may have important repercussions for the quality of the last years of life.

2. A second set of contingencies affecting life for the elderly includes adequate finances, shelter, and medical care. The extent to which these are problems depends both upon the composition of the older population and the degree of societal support. Consider first the changes noted above. Between the first and third cohorts there is a tremendous change in educational level, financial preparedness for old age, and ability to function effectively in a complex society. Then combine these changes in cohort characteristics with the greatly expanded role of government in providing social welfare for the needy. The effect is that the notorious problems of old age, poverty and poor health, must necessarily have lost much of their force. No one would argue that these problems have disappeared, but neither should one minimize the significance of the decline in these problems and the anticipated further decline in coming years.

3. A third factor is the provision of recreation or leisure facilities. Recently a good deal of attention has been directed toward the need for leisure activities for the aged. But leisure activities cannot be made the major developmental task for the last stage of life. Why, at the end of life, should we encourage individuals to concentrate upon goalless and trivial activities? An emphasis upon leisure fits best the unfortunate view of old age as a purposeless time to be filled with insignificant activities while one waits for death. As Comfort (1976) puts it, this emphasis "childrenizes older people." The 1.7 million persons reaching age 65 this year, most of whom are healthy and intelligent, deserve better advice than this for the 15 years (on average) they have ahead of them.

4. The final factor Butler lists is the need for societal provision of adequate social roles, and above all this is the conclusion of this paper. Unfortunately, the trend over this century has been to remove older people from constructive roles and to encourage the waste of their resources. But the new cohorts entering old age are increasingly able to make substantial contributions to societal welfare. The greatest challenge with respect to the older population is

now to provide social roles in which they are encouraged to
accept new responsibilities for constructive activities.

If creative thought is given to this problem, a variety
of appropriate, stimulating, and feasible roles for the elderly can be developed. Let me suggest just one area deserving further attention--designing ways for the elderly to meet
geriatric needs. Younger-old persons are freed from many responsibilities in the labor force and in the family, and they
have many of the resources needed to meet the needs of the
older-old. The younger-old are closest to the older-old in
life course experiences, and hence may have a deeper understanding of this population. And the need for persons to
care for the older-old population is expanding. In 1940
there were 1.4 persons over age 70 for every person aged 65-
69. In 1970 this ratio increased to 1.8, and by 2000 there
will be 2.4 persons over 70 for each person aged 65-69. The
development of this type of role, along with other constructive roles, is the direction that social policy concerned
with the aged should increasingly take.

References

Butler, Robert N. 1974. Successful aging and the role of
the life review. The Journal of the American Geriatric
Society.

Comfort, Alexander. 1976. Age prejudice in America. Social
Policy 7:3–8.

Harris, Louis, and Associates, Inc. 1975. The Myth and
Reality of Aging in America. Washington, D.C.: The
National Council on the Aging.

Neugarten, Bernice L. et al. 1965. Age norms, age constraints and adult socialization. American Journal of
Sociology 70:710–717.

Neugarten, Bernice L. and Gunhild O. Hagstead. 1976. Age
and the life course. In Robert Binstock and Ethel
Shanas, eds.; The Handbook of Aging and the Social
Sciences. New York: Van Nostrand Reinhold Co.

Pratt, Henry J. 1976. The Gray Lobby. Chicago: The University of Chicago Press.

Riley, Matilda White. 1976. Age strata in social systems.
In Robert Binstock and Ethel Shanas, eds.; The Handbook
of Aging and the Social Sciences. New York: Van
Nostrand Reinhold Co.

Riley, Matilda White, Marilyn Johnson, and Anne Foner. 1972.
A Sociology of Age Stratification. New York: Russell
Sage Foundation.

What with Inflation and Unemployment, Who Can Afford to Retire?

James N. Morgan

Great issues of public policy are being discussed, and decisions are being made today in the face of massive ignorance about the situations, desires, plans, or expectations of the individual people affected. And a false crisis, composed of lack of economic understanding by some and a focus on the wrong economic issues by others, has led to ill-advised and partial changes in the Social Security System and suggestions for further changes, including changes in the retirement age rules.

Background in the Social Security System

Frightening phrases like "bankruptcy of the system", "exhaustion of the trust fund" and "trillions of unfunded liability" imply that people cannot count on getting their Social Security benefits, even though they are a government obligation. While some charge that the Social Security system is a "bad buy" for individuals because they get so little back, others charge that it is unsound because it promises more than it can pay, and the contradiction goes unchallenged. Similar contradictions appear when some urge early retirement to free up jobs for younger people and others urge later retirement so a surplus will build up in the Social Security accounts or because people want to keep working.

I shall not attempt to clear up the basic economics of retirement annuities here, but let me say just enough to indicate a proper analysis: The system could not have built up a full fund and accrued interest on it like a private annuity. If it had, the contributions to the fund would have depressed the economy, and their investment would have left the government owning much of American industry. Instead, we invented a kind of "pay as you go" logic to justify giving pensions to older cohorts who had not fully paid for them. Now people insist that the payroll tax cover all benefits, without asking whether people should not be credited with some interest if they contribute to the system for forty years or so of working life and if they receive benefits spread over some fifteen years of retirement. In a private annuity of this sort, at a modest 3 per cent real interest rate, 60 per cent of what you got back would represent interest on your savings. We could therefore justify the use of some general tax money to pay part of the Social Security benefits, representing the equivalent of the interest we should be earning on those payroll contributions if they were invested. If the actuarial accounting is done properly, then, each cohort is already close to paying its own way in terms of its contributions and expected benefits.

Retirement Situations and Attitudes

I want to talk about people and their situations and desires because the so-called "Social Security crisis" (drummed up by its critics and the newspapers and people who understand no economics) has led some to suggest that we raise the retirement age, at the very time when massive and persistent unemployment has led others to suggest encouraging early retirement. We are short on fact, but we do know that there has been a massive increase in the number of people wanting jobs—arising from the maturing of the post-war baby boom cohorts, from legal and illegal immigration, and from the entrance of a much larger fraction of women into the labor market. In fact we know that ever since the Social Security allowed people to retire before 65 at actuarially reduced benefits, the vast majority have done so. And when in 1973 those in the Social Security Retirement History Survey who were already retired were asked about returning to work, more than half said their health precluded or limited it, and only ten per cent said they both could return to work and wanted to do so. (Motley, 1977). That panel sample includes only the younger among the retired (aged 62-67 in 1973 and retired since 1969). So mandatory retirement is not having any substantial impact. Nor did gradual retirement appear to be something to be encouraged. Analysis of the 9 per cent in the Retirement History Survey sample who retired gradually indicated that they were mostly low-income people whose part-time work provided needed income. Nor were they happier than other retirees. (Schwab, 1977). So gradual retirement does not apparently ease the transition into retirement. Discouraging retirement might mean more unemployment, not more happiness.

Some economists will tell you that in theory unemployment should never be a problem when there are unmet needs in the world; it is simply a matter of figuring out how to allow those needs to be expressed in the market (with money) and to put people to work meeting them. But it is not that easy and in the meantime we do have unemployment, and underemployment, combined with inflation.

It would help us in thinking about such problems to know some facts. As usual, the "action people" are sure they know all the important facts, and they can cite individual cases to prove it. And as usual, researchers like myself are convinced that we know very little and need a lot more information before we can understand the

situation and make sensible policy to fit.

I want to focus on the retirement decision as a crucial element in all this. When people retire is bound to depend on their desires, and on their ability to afford it, and on the constraints and regulations they face. We cannot extrapolate from the past and present to the future in this area because we have been seeing massive changes from year to year and, hence, in the lifetime experiences of different cohorts. We have had inflation, unemployment, and large erratic changes in asset values. Traditional hedges against inflation like the stock market have failed us. House prices have risen more than 10 per cent a year for a decade and a half, providing many with large capital gains which they cannot use to pay the food or medical bills, and which are accompanied by increased out-of-pocket costs such as insurance and taxes. Rumor has it that some whose houses have gone up in value are trying to "eat their capital gains" by taking out larger mortgages, borrowing on the house, and spending the money. Like most such dramatic stories, this is probably rare in fact.

We cannot even reconstruct past trends in earnings of individuals because in the available cross-section data, average earnings, (at least among the less educated), appear to fall after about age 50, yet most people's individual earnings actually continue to rise until they retire. Cross-section age patterns do not give cohort experience, particularly when real and money wages are rising over time, as Herman Miller pointed out years ago.

Careful investigations of individual patterns of earnings, accumulations, and retirement require longitudinal studies, but those take a lot of money and, even more important, take a lot of time before they produce data. In the interim, we need cheaper and faster studies to furnish information that can be used right now, both to improve planning and to provide the benchmark measures for longitudinal studies.

Three approaches are possible: (1) we can make some cautious but useful comparisons among age groups in a cross-section, (2) we can ask some retrospective questions about the retirement process, and (3) we can use repeated inexpensive cross-section sample surveys to monitor changes in people's retirement provisions, plans, and expectations.

Some Suggestive Research Findings

We have already asked some questions of the retired about why they retired when they did, and how they feel about it. (Barfield and Morgan, 1978-a and 1978-b). The results show that health, money, and regulations are all that matter. People retire because they have to or because they can afford to. They may have to because of bad health or a compulsory retirement age. But if they can afford to, most will retire and even do it early. The picture of someone dragged unwillingly into retirement is true only for professionals, a few others who enjoy their work, and those who are reluctant because they need the money!

Our earlier study conducted in 1966 (Barfield and Morgan, 1969) found little evidence of desire to keep working. It also found a dominance of economic factors in retirement. Those who retired early did so because their health or the job gave out, or because they found they could afford it, and plans to retire early were dominated by economic expectations of ability to afford it, including having the mortgage paid off and no children still to be educated. We indicated at the time a possible polarization between, on the one hand, those who retired early—or at least willingly—because they could afford it and those, on the other hand, who retired unwillingly—inadequately financed—because of illness, obsolescent skills or mandatory retirement. We have been unable to fund longitudinal studies to test whether this trend is indeed appearing today.

Certain clues to the trend can be obtained by comparing age groups in a single cross-section. For example, the plans and expectations of those not yet retired can be compared with the reports of those already retired. True, they are different cohorts, but when we found, as we did, that substantial numbers of those still working said they expected to do more volunteer work when they retired, but that retired people did not report doing more volunteer work than before they retired, we can justifiably suspect that those expectations are naive.

More important, when age differences appear, as they did in 1966, in the proportion who said they planned to retire early, with the younger people more likely to plan early retirement, we can speculate whether that means people get more realistic as they age, or whether it means that each succeeding cohort is less imbued with the work ethic. Do those closer to age 65 have less expectation of early retirement because they are older, or because they were born in a generation that saw the depression and were taught that work is good?

The obvious next step was to remeasure retirement plans after the passage of time. We had two alternative hypotheses. First, if the decline in the propensity to plan early retirement with age was a pure age effect, the same pattern according to current age should reappear. Second, if it were a pure trend, with each succeeding cohort persistently less interested in work and more interested in early retirement, then the whole curve should shift forward, the 50 year olds of 1975 looking like the 40 year olds of 1965, for example, because both represent the same cohort (or generation).

So we had two questions—(1) what the current cross-section age patterns would tell us about how to interpret the age patterns of

1965, and (2) what inflation, unemployment, and fluctuating values of people's invested savings were doing to retirement plans.

What appeared was a curious change in the pattern of early retirement plans across age groups. Neither hypothesis was true. The pattern did not stay the same, reflecting pure age differences, nor did it shift forward, representing a trend across cohorts or the effect of inflation. Instead it developed a kink. The 50-60 year old cohort (in 1975) seemed to retain its earlier frequent expectation of early retirement, but the younger cohort did not have proportionately higher percentages planning to retire early. To be sure, the sample is small, the historic time a difficult one of confusion and uncertainty, and the related data on financial provision inadequate, but the intriguing possibility of a third hypothesis remains.

In line with this third hypothesis, it would appear that there is a cohort, now approaching retirement, which had a particularly favorable historic experience. They entered the labor market in an upswing, achieving status, seniority and job security before the unemployment of the 1970's hit. But the next cohort entered the labor market in a less ebullient phase, when they had to compete with the maturing results of the post-war baby boom and the entrance of many more women into the labor market. Also, government policies were more concerned with inflation than with unemployment. Even if unemployment did not hit each one of them, it may have affected their sense of security. And their speed of promotion has been and may continue to be slower.

After them is coming still another cohort, now too young for us to have asked them about their retirement plans—they may not have any yet—who may in turn be much better off and able to retire early. They are marrying later, having fewer children and mostly marrying a partner who also works most of the time, and they are a smaller cohort. Indeed, the very cause of the concern about their capacity to pay for the Social Security retirement benefits of the more numerous older cohorts really means that they will have good employment and earning prospects because they have less competition in getting good jobs. In this cohort, people are scarce! (Easterlin's focus on the relative size of succeeding cohorts may be useful, but with relative size affecting early retirement even more than it affects birthrates! Strumpel, Thornton, and Curtin, 1976).

There are intriguing data from other studies on the attitudes of different age groups that tie in with our notion that different cohorts may reflect different historic experience. In Britain and America, concern with financial security seems to decrease with each succeeding cohort, as each has less and less direct memory of the Great Depression. An exception is a cohort aged 50 to 59 in 1974 who worry less about financial security perhaps because they have more of it than most. (Inglehart, 1977).

Socioeconomic Change
and Retirement Age

When people want to and can afford to retire may well be subject to waves of change. If so, it is important to find out a great deal more than we now know before we make permanent alterations in the mandatory retirement age, or in the Social Security system. We desperately need information on people's accumulations of pension rights and assets, and on their expectations about income, family needs, future accumulation, and work and retirement. If we confronted these expectations with some expert judgments on whether they are likely to be proven right or wrong, we might have a better base for policy. We need to know whether the patterns of the Retirement History Study will continue or not.

Similarly, we are deficient of information, except from the mostly retired cohorts of the Social Security Administration's Retirement History Study, about the extent to which people really want to keep working, as distinct from wanting to keep eating. It is not enough to ask people whether they want to work, because working means money. If they want to be busy and useful, as distinct from needing money, why is there so little volunteer work done by the retired? One might reply that the worth of an activity tends to be gauged by whether it is paid for, and that accepting pay might lose a person his/her Social Security benefits, but the nagging suspicion remains that older people mostly prefer leisure to work so long as they can afford it.

The Process of Retiring

But what about the process itself, apart from determinants of the age of retirement? We can learn much from watching how people retire, the efforts they make to try alternatives other than staying with the main job or simply retiring. And we can study this process retrospectively by asking people to recall it since the decisions were major and salient. The main memory biases will be not in reports of final earnings and savings and the economics of retirement, but in reports of how the person felt about retiring, how much effort went into finding other employment if retirement from the main job was compulsory, and how much declining health and energy was involved. But major illnesses, spells of unemployment before retirement, and actual other jobs held are recoverable from memory. The alternative options available, and their economic implications, should also be ascertainable retrospectively. Most people who retire know what retiring a year or two earlier or later would do to their retirement income. If they did not, such a finding would itself raise questions about whether to allow actuarial increases in retirement income from Social Security for those retiring at age 66 or 67. Would such increases really affect people's retirement decisions if they didn't know what their new options were?

We desperately need regular, repeated surveys to monitor changes in people's plans and provisions for retirement. It seems incredible that we are making massive changes in Social Security and proposing changes in retirement regulations in almost total absence of information about what people want or what their situations are. Aside from our own studies, and a few retirement questions asked of the older labor force panels analyzed at Ohio State (Parnes, 1970-74), we have only the Social Security Administration's records, their one study of a panel now mostly retired, and their surveys of newly entitled beneficiaries. None of this gives any adequate "lead time" for monitoring of changes. We know from Social Security data that the vast majority retire early, and have done so ever since they were allowed to (even though at actuarially reduced benefits). We have some evidence that some of them "had to"—indicated by prior irregularity of earnings or by unemployment experience or illness-disability. Our own data indicate that others voluntarily retired early because they could afford to. It is important to know whether this polarity continues, with two opposite groups retiring early.

It is even more important in discussions of retirement age to know how many really want to work past 65, apart from a need for money, and how many want to and can afford to retire early; and we need to know whether the two groups are in entirely different occupations. We might see the highly skilled and productive retiring early while the unskilled who need the money keep working.

We are including some questions in the eleventh wave of our Panel Study of Family Income Dynamics (spring 1978), asking non-retired respondents over age 50 about retirement plans and expectations about pensions, and asking the retired about how voluntary and satisfactory that process was. We could not cover the full financial details of assets and retirement equities, but we can combine the earlier panel data on work and earnings histories with the replies to these few questions about retirement plans or experiences.

The Economics of Retirement

Given the massive effects of changing retirement age on employment, productivity, unemployment, and the flows of funds into and out of pension funds and Social Security, it seems incredible that we know so little about the facts. It is easy and common to say we need studies, and it always seems self-serving for us data collectors to urge more, but in this particular instance the need for empirical studies seems urgent and obvious. Whatever else these studies cover, they must deal with economics. A series of studies have shown that economic factors dominate not only the decision to retire, but people's satisfaction with retirement. (Barfield and Morgan, 1969, 1970 1978-a and b; Chatfield, 1977; Edwards and Klemmack, 1973). Only health rivals money as a determinant of satisfaction, and we have already gone a long way to deal with health problems, particularly of the aged.

The economics of age of retirement is of course crucial, not just for the money-flows of the Social Security system, but for an individual's retirement benefits even when actuarially computed. For example, assume the average person works and accumulates for forty years and has an expected retirement period of fifteen years. Now suppose his life expectancy increases by two years. By working one additional year at the old contribution rates, he can provide for the remaining additional year of retirement. The reason is, of course, that working one more year benefits in three ways: one more year's contribution to retirement funds, one more year's interest accumulation on the huge fund already accumulated (or at least that would have been accumulated if Social Security were "funded"), and one less year of expected retirement. By the same token, to make a person work an extra year for the same retirement benefits is a very large financial imposition on him or her.

A study of people's financial provisions for retirement would of course have to cover the whole field of wealth and wealth accumulation, which is something we need to know more about anyway. We have had a period of overall prosperity in the United States for many years, but accompanied by unemployment and continued poverty and wildly gyrating asset values. The result may well have been increased inequality of wealth, but we do not know. We may also have an historically unprecedented number of people approaching retirement age with more wealth than they can possibly need for themselves the rest of their lives. What these fortunate people do in managing and ultimately disposing of that wealth is crucial in many ways. There were asset data collected in the older male panel of the National Longitudinal Study, and in the 1972-73 Consumer Expenditure Survey, though neither attempted to value insurance or pension equities. (Parnes, 1970-74).

What has inhibited studies of wealth has been a concern that accurate wealth data could not be secured from individuals and families, and validity of studies made twenty years ago seemed to show difficulties. But things have changed. Most asset incomes now have to be reported to the Internal Revenue Service, by the source paying the interest or dividends or rent, and in all cases assigned to some taxpayer (Social Security number) individually. We have also learned some things about interviewing and securing cooperation from respondents. There are now precedents and procedures for statistical studies that combine interview data with data from various records and files to increase coverage and accuracy. Finally, for many purposes, precision in measuring wealth is less important than better reports on how it was accumulated, its portfolio distributions, how the investments are managed, and what people plan to do with it. Without expecting too much from even the best designed data collections, we can surely improve our information from its abysmal state.

Another reason for continuing to monitor and study people's

retirement plans, provisions, and decisions is to see the economic result of other massive social changes. Many of the places where we work are no longer nice places to live (if they ever were), and burgeoning developments for "good living" are appearing in places where there are few employment opportunities. At the same time, more and more of us end up owning a home before we retire, with all the emotional attachment and unwillingness to pay even partial capital gains taxes. If people are to move when they retire, they mostly have to plan and search, and start making commitments, and such activities can be studied.

For those with a house paid for, but running short of current income to pay for food and medical bills and property taxes, some have suggested the government should offer a lifetime annuity to be paid for in the end by selling the house after both owners are deceased. It would be a useful and relatively simple piece of research to ask a representative sample of older home owners whether they might opt for such an alternative. One could ask how they think their children would feel about losing the family home, and also ask a representative sample of younger people how they would feel if their parents willed their home to the government in return for a supplemental lifetime annuity. The offer could be made realistic by providing the respondents with an estimate of the amount they could expect each month (a) from such a housing annuity, or (b) if they sold their house and rented a dwelling with part of the resulting annuity. And to make the offer still more realistic and fair, the annuity could be adjusted for future inflation, as a way of letting the people rather than the government benefit from those capital gains on their homes that accompany inflation. The initial annuity, using a real 3 per cent interest rate net of any inflation, would be looked up in a table like that given below.

TABLE 1
Monthly Annuity Payable
With or Without Continued Occupancy of Home

	Continued Occupancy, Title Transfers When Both are Dead			Annuity Purchasable by Selling Home now and Renting		
	Age of Husband when Annuity Starts			Age of Husband when Annuity Starts		
Net Equity in House, at Start	60	65	70	60	65	70
$ 10,000	$ 31	$ 45	$ 73	$ 56	$ 70	$ 98
20,000	62	90	145	112	140	196

TABLE 1 (CONT.)

Monthly Annuity Payable
With or Without Continued Occupancy of Home

	Continued Occupancy, Title Transfers When Both are Dead			Annuity Purchasable by Selling Home now and Renting		
	Age of Husband when Annuity Starts			Age of Husband when Annuity Starts		
Net Equity in House, at Start	60	65	70	60	65	70
30,000	93	135	219	168	210	294
40,000	124	180	292	224	280	392
50,000	155	225	365	280	349	488
------	---	---	---	---	---	---
$ 100,000	310	448	727	560	698	977

Annuity continues at 2/3rds amount if one spouse dies, is adjusted proportionately as cost of living rises. If occupants must move out, e.g., to a nursing home, annuity would be increased to reflect the gain from immediate sale of house. Based on 3% rate of interest.

Finally, and perhaps most interesting of all, we have a massive increase in the proportion of aging couples where both are working. Since men tend to be married to women several years younger than they are, even though women tend to live six years longer, it is clear that decisions about the retirement of two working spouses will involve some problems. Either they will retire at different times, with problems about the usual post-retirement travel (and change of residence), or one will have to retire early, or one will have to retire late. Something has to give. Social Security may not look so bad to women if they want to retire early on their own benefits while their husband keeps on working, or if they keep on working and accumulating higher benefits after the husband is retired.

In all this, it is useful to have comparisons with age groups just beginning to think about the problem, those in the middle, and those mostly looking back and evaluating their decisions.

Summary

I have not focused much on what we know about retirement, because of an overwhelming sense that we know very little and most of that is rapidly becoming out of date and irrelevant. We are in desperate need of better information, not just to understand human behavior and condition, but to illuminate and guide policies about Social Security, retirement age, and related issues.

References

Barfield, Richard, and Morgan, James. Early Retirement, the Decision and the Experience, and A Second Look. Ann Arbor, Michigan: Institute for Social Research, The University of Michigan, (reprinted together in 1974).

Barfield, Richard, and Morgan, James. 1978-a. "Trends in Planned Early Retirement", The Gerontologist 18 (February): 13-18.

Barfield, Richard, and Morgan, James. 1978-b. "Trends in Satisfaction with Retirement," The Gerontologist, 18 (February): 19-23.

Chatfield, Walter F. 1977. "Economic and Sociological Factors Influencing Life Satisfaction of the Aged," Journal of Gerontology 32 (September): 593-599.

Edwards, J. and Klemmack, L. 1973. "Correlates of Life Satisfaction: A Reexamination," Journal of Gerontology 28 : 297-302.

Inglehart, Ronald. 1977. The Silent Revolution. Princeton: The Princeton University Press.

Motley, Dena K. 1977. The Availability of Retirees for Return to Work, a paper presented at the San Francisco meetings of the Gerontological Society, November.

Parnes, Herbert, et al. 1970-74. The Pre-Retirement Years. Washington, D.C.: U.S. Department of Labor, Manpower Monographs, Vol. 1, Vol. 3, Vol. 4.

Schulz, James H. 1976. "Income Distribution and the Aging." In Robert H. Binstock and Ethel Shanas, eds. Handbook of aging and the Social Sciences. New York: Van Nostrand Reinhold.

Schwab, Karen A. 1977. Gradual Retirement and Adjustment in Retirement, a paper presented at the San Francisco meetings of the Gerontological Society, November.

Sherman, Sally. 1973. "Assets on the Threshold of Retirement." Social Security Bulletin (August).

Strumpel, Burkhard, Thornton, Arland, and Curtin, Richard T. 1976. Fertility Change after the Baby Boom: The Role of Economic Stress, Female Employment, and Education. Ann Arbor, Michigan: Institute for Social Research, The University of Michigan.

10

Prospects for Aging in America

Theodore J. Gordon

Introduction

Progress in increasing human life expectancy was pain-
fully slow until this century, when advances in medicine and
sanitation produced a dramatic rise. In 1900 the average
age at death in the United States was about 48 years. Today,
the average age at death is about 72-77 for women and 68 for
men. As a result we have large numbers of people reaching
old age for the first time in history. In 1900 about 3
million Americans were age 65 or over, about 1 in 25. Today
about 22 million Americans are, 1 in 10. With current mortality this figure is expected to rise to at least 31 million
by the year 2000, when perhaps 1 in 8 Americans will be age
65 or more. The primary reason for the increase in life
expectany has been the success in controlling the infectious
diseases that used to kill before middle age. Today few
people die from such diseases as tuberculosis, pneumonia, in-
fluenza, or typhoid fever, which used to claim many lives in
childhood and young adulthood.

While life expectancy at birth has increased appreciably
since the turn of the century, life expectancy at advanced
age has improved much less. Yet there is reason to believe
that this pattern may change considerably in the future. Extensive research is now being directed toward finding a cure
for diseases that cause death among the aged and toward
reaching an understanding of the mechanism of aging itself,
the outcome of which might provide the means for modulating
the rate of aging. In addition, progress is being made in
the development of advanced non-biological prosthesis.
Breakthroughs in any of these domains could alter the expected mortality of the population, particularly among older
cohorts in society. Extensions of life expectancy of the
elderly already are taking place, and the trend seems to be
accelerating.

With the possibility in view of increasing life span and life expectancy by curing diseases or by a direct frontal attack on aging, it is appropriate to ask about potential consequences of such developments. Just what techniques can be expected and when? How expensive and generally available are they likely to be? How will their benefits be distributed? For those developments that seem likely, what will be the impact on demography, the economy, welfare, and a host of other factors relating to our society? For example, how would the labor force be affected? Or social security? Or attitudes toward death and dying? Or the family? To what extent should the government or special interest groups provide incentives or disincentives to accomplish these changes? (This is an issue already raised by the demonstrated correlation between cigarette smoking and lung cancer.) Indeed, is increased longevity a goal toward which public and private resources should be channeled?

The Futures Group recently performed a research study that bears directly on these topics.[1] The study was a technology assessment of life-extending technologies and was designed not only to explore the technologies which could provide extended life, but to reach a deeper understanding of the impacts of these developments. We found that life expectancy is increasing, that new biomedical technologies would accelerate this trend, and that changing age distribution would indeed have significant economic and social impact. In this paper I plan to summarize some of the principal findings of this work.

We did not attempt to answer all of the questions prospective extension raises. Time and other resources were too

---

[1] This work was performed under contract to the Applied Research Directorate (RANN) of the National Science Foundation; it was funded at a level of about $300,000 and extended over a period of 18 months. The participants in this study, other than the author, included Herbert Gerjuoy, Mark Anderson, John Stover, and Jackson Davis, all of The Futures Group staff. Thus, the concepts and findings of the study, reported in this paper, represent the work of all of these people. Furthermore, a large number of consultants and interview respondents provided essential information, judgments, and assistance to the study team. The Institute of Society, Ethics, and the Life Sciences provided substantial assistance in the field of values and ethics; the American Council of Life Insurance also made a valuable contribution to this work by conducting a symposium on the impact of life extension on the insurance industry.

limited, but more importantly, many of these issues, by their nature, have no answer. They are, will be, and ought to be matters of public choice. This work hopefully provides some information that can illiminate the issues and inform public discussion about what aging will come to mean--biologically and socially--in the years ahead.

Study Design

After first defining the state-of-the-art of life extending technologies through literature search, interviews, and contributions from consultants the study focused on generating forecasts of the future of biomedical technologies that could affect life span and life expectancy. How might they evolve? What are the important prospective breakthroughs? When might they occur? What paces them? What would their consequences be for life extension? These forecasts were derived using in-depth interviews with a carefully selected panel of 25 experts.

The technologies forecasted and their expected impacts on life expectancy covered a very broad range. The study team chose to group the technologies into sets and to form several scenarios based on these sets. Other non-technology assumptions also were made; these were consistent with the scenario themes. In effect, the scenarios formed alternative "worlds," each based on different life-extending technologies and concomitant assumptions. The remainder of the study was devoted to an identification of the consequences of the assumptions contained in the scenarios. Demographic, economic, social, political, and value consequences were derived for each of the scenarios.

A computer simulation was used in the various scenarios to interpret the survival curves in terms of their consequences for demography. Labor force estimates were made on the basis of the demographic forecasts and plausible assumptions about participation rates. Economic impacts were evaluated using an economic model. Estimates of social security in-flow and out-flow were also made. All of these impacts were quantitative; non-quantitative impacts were also studied. A symposium was held to inquire about the consequences for insurance of assumptions about life extension. In-depth interviews with sociologists and social gerontologists were held to identify a spectrum of potential social changes flowing from life extension. Papers on values and ethical issues were prepared and reviewed by The Institute of Society, Ethics, and the Life Sciences.

EFFECT OF CURVE SQUARING AND LIFE-EXTENDING TECHNOLOGIES

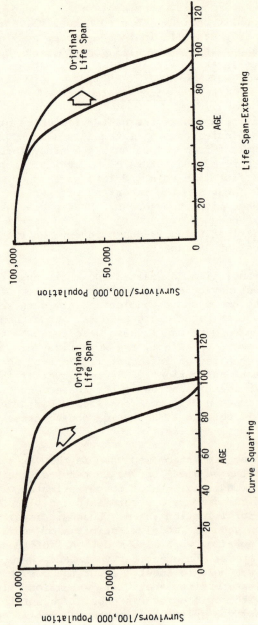

Source: The Futures Group

Figure 1

Now the problem was: how are the forecasted impacts likely to be perceived by the interest groups? Of course, such judgments are value-laden and multidimensional. An impact seen as good by one group might be seen as bad by another. These matters were among the most difficult to address during this study. For a third time in the study, in-depth interviews were utilized, this time with selected representatives of interest groups to explore the perceived consequences and desirability of a range of impacts of life-extending technologies.

Finally, we reviewed the research product and on the basis of our findings and projections, recommended certain actions which, it seemed to us, promised to improve the future situation.

Curve Squaring vs. Span Extending

In our interviews of biomedical experts, we found that there were three general strategies being pursued.

- Research into the prevention, diagnosis and treatment of heart disease, cancer, and stroke.

- Research into the cause for aging itself, with the possibility of slowing the rate of aging.

- Research into the relationship among social conditions, aging, and death.

The effects of these technologies could be viewed as either increasing the number of people who live to older age (squaring the survival curve) or increasing the maximum age to which people live (life span extending). The kinds of societies that are produced by these two types of technologies are quite different. In the case of curve squaring, more people of middle age live to old age, but death rate inevitably accelerates as maximum life span is approached. For the technologies which have the sole effect of increasing life span, more individuals live past what is regarded as maximum age today (Figure 1).

It is hard to conceive of a purely curve squaring technology that would not have some effect on life span as well, and vice versa. For example, any process that tended to square the survival curve by eliminating death due to heart disease might well be expected in addition to extend life span in individuals whose aging is due partly to reduced oxygen and nutrient supply to tissues because of failing cardiac function.

Biomedical Technologies

The biomedical experts who were interviewed during this study were asked to provide judgments about technologies that could affect life expectancy. They were presented with lists of potential developments (which we had obtained through a literature search), asked to add to the list, asked to judge the probability of occurrence of developments with which they were familiar or experienced and, finally, to judge the consequences of the developments, if they were to occur, on survival. The technologies could be divided into two principal classes: those that would have the effect of squaring the survival curve and those that would extend life span. Curve squaring technologies can be divided into the five following categories:

1. Cardiovascular disease prevention, diagnosis, and treatment.
2. Cerebrovascular disease prevention, diagnosis, and treatment.
3. Malignant neoplastic disease prevention, diagnosis, and treatment.
4. Non-biological prosthesis.
5. Improvements in the environment, such as those that reduce stress.

For the most part the technologies that the group felt represented likely improvements in these domains are summarized in Table 1.

The life span extending technologies forecasted by the group can be divided into the following four categories:

1. Technologies that alter cellular aging processes such as dietary control or supplementation.
2. Technologies that alter aging of organ systems such as the reticuloendothelial system.
3. Technologies that alter aging induced by organ systems such as hormone-induced aging.
4. Tissue regeneration technologies.

Table 2 summarizes the principal concepts and approaches to the control of aging that were enumerated by the panel. Other key findings of this inquiry are presented in Table 3.

The life span extension technologies will require breakthroughs, and it would be surprising if aging control is demonstrated for human beings over the next two decades. This is not to say that we believe control of aging is impossible or unlikely quite the contrary, we think that many of

Table 1

LIFE-EXTENDING TECHNOLOGIES
JUDGED MORE LIKELY THAN NOT BY
THE YEAR 2000

- Kidney transplantation.

- Non-biological heart or blood vessel prosthesis.

- Non-biological kidney prosthesis.

- Cerebrovascular disease prevention by pharmacological means.

- Cardiovascular disease prevention by pharmacological means.

- Control of aging by control of diet.

- Cardiovascular disease treatment by heart, or blood vessel surgery.

- Control of aging by control of foreign protein rejection.

- Cardiovascular disease prevention by lifestyle control.

- Cardiovascular disease diagnosis by transmission or reflection analysis.

- Cardiovascular disease diagnosis by energy or work output analysis.

- Control of aging of the endocrine system.

- Control of aging by control of hormones that induce aging.

- Cardiovascular disease emergency care.

- Heart or blood-vessel transplantation.

- Malignant neoplasm diagnosis by internal probes.

- Cardiovascular disease diagnosis by internal probes.

- Malignant neoplasm prevention by electromagnetic means.

- Control of aging by control of self-recognition.

- Cardiovascular disease treatment by chemotherapy.

- Malignant neoplasm diagnosis by transmission or reflection analysis.

- Cardiovascular disease prevention by immunological means.

- Control of aging by control of cultural factors.

- Cerebrovascular disease treatment by general support.

- Malignant neoplasm treatment by surgery.

- Cardiovascular disease prevention by genetic means.

- Tissue regeneration by electromagnetic means.

- Cardiovascular disease treatment by lifestyle control.

- Cerebrovascular disease diagnosis by chemical analysis.

- Immunological control of aging.

- Cerebrovascular disease prevention by lifestyle control.

- Cerebrovascular disease diagnosis by transmission or reflection analysis.

- Bone, joint, or tooth transplantation.

- Malignant neoplasm treatment by chemotherapy.

- Cerebrovascular disease diagnosis using general appearance or complaints.

Table 2

PRINCIPAL CONCEPTS AND APPROACHES TO CONTROL OF AGING

- Effects of diet: growth of rats and other laboratory animals can be retarded by control of protein or caloric content of their diet.

- Lowering temperature: scientists have extended the life span of the fruit fly and species of fish by lowering the temperature of their environment.

- The immune mechanism: some researchers believe the central factor in aging is the progressive failure of the immune mechanism.

- The pituitary: it has been suggested that the pituitary produces a hormone that programs dying; early studies have shown that whole pituitary extract can prolong the life span of old rats.

- Loss of tissue elasticity: some researchers have emphasized the increasing stiffness of connective tissue with increasing chronological age; many of the effects of aging can be shown to be secondary consequences of loss of tissue elasticity.

- Cross-linkage: molecular cross-linking agents within the cell can induce symptoms similar to those of senescence; these agents may impair the genetic replication mechanism.

- Insoluble end-product accumulation: pigments such as lipofuscin accumulate in cells as they age; the closely related substance, ceroid, as been linked to neuron degeneration and death.

- Free radicals: these are very energetic molecular fragments generally produced by high energy events in the cytoplasm; they apparently interfere with cellular metabolism. If the high energy event occurs within the cell nucleus and affects genetic material, the genetic record itself may be affected.

- Abnormal oxidation: such processes may reduce cellular metabolic and immunological functioning; progressive oxidation of fatty components of the cell membrane may explain why older cells are more vulnerable to attack by the body's own immunological defenses.

- Cellular replication errors: some researchers have emphasized the importance to aging of the incidence of noise in the transcription of genetic information.

- Membrane damage: the notion that aging may be a consequence of damage to membrane surrounding lysosomes is a proposed basis for the reported anti-aging effects of membrane stabilizing drugs.

- Cell division limit: some laboratory test have indicated that human-derived cells have a finite reproductive capacity which allows one to predict the growth, senescence, and death of an in vitro cell population.

Table 3
BIOMEDICAL FORECASTS--KEY FINDINGS

- Largely distinct lines of technological progress
  would lead to curve squaring as opposed to span
  extension achievements.

- Competing strategic approaches to technological
  advances are

  ° Immortalist: aim at conquering aging
  ° Incrementalist: continue traditional
    step-by-step biomedical progress
  ° Meliorist: improve the general life
    situation of the elderly

- Competing theories of aging may be classed
  broadly as based on programmed aging or on
  gradual wearing out of the body; on intra-
  cellular or on organ system processes.

- Competing theories of aging well may be all true
  insofar as they identify limiting factors; at
  issue is which limiting factors most narrowly
  limit survival and vigor.

- Curve squaring progress will depend primarily on

  ° Public health education
  ° Environmental control
  ° Advances in dealing with key diseases
    (cardiovascular disease, cerebrovascular
    disease, and cancer)

- The effects of life span extension will make
  themselves felt only well into the next century,
  as people who benefit from span extending technologies start to reach advanced chronological
  age.

- The introduction of life span extending technologies will be accompanied at first by great
  uncertainty about the amount of span extension
  to be anticipated.

- Deterioration in the environment and synergized
  unhealthful impacts of various kinds of environmental deterioration could lead to the opposite
  of curve squaring--fewer individuals surviving
  to their full span.

the lines of research that are being pursued are promising.
However, this work is being conducted at a very basic level
and there is no shared perception about the basic mechanisms
for aging.   Thus, scientists engaged in this work are following many different leads. Demonstration and validation of
one or another of these theories will take time.

Scenarios

Seven scenarios were defined in the study.   Each
differed in assumptions about the advent of life-extending
technologies and concomitant factors.   Some principal dimensions of these scenarios (and their demographic consequences)
are summarized in Table 4.   These scenarios were designed to
encompass a large but plausible range of assumptions about
biomedical technologies; they were used as the basis for examining the spectrum of impacts that might be expected to
flow from the introduction of new biomedical techniques.
None of the scenarios should be viewed as a forecast; rather,
we believe that the real world will lie somewhere within the
range defined by these cases. More specifically, among the
impacts examined were impacts on the labor force, the economy,
social security, insurance (health, life, and annuities),
society (e.g., family and inheritance patterns), interest
groups, and values and ethics.

FACTORS	SCENARIO						
	1Z	1	1A	2	2A	3	3A
Life Span Extending Technologies	None	None	None	15 Years Added	15 Years Added	90 Years Added	90 Years Added
Curve Squaring Technologies	Desquared	None	Yes	None	Yes	None	Yes
Fertility (births per women of child-bearing age)	2.5	2.5	2.1	2.5	2.1	2.5	2.1

Table 4.   Summary of Scenario Assumptions

In preparing these scenarios age-specific female to male
mortality rates were assumed (basically an extension of
trends which have existed since the start of the century--
although in scenarios 3 and 3A we included a test of a re-
versal of those trends), and migration (assumed to remain
constant at 400,000 per year).

The total fertility rate was defined by each of the
scenario descriptions as either remaining at replacement
level (scenarios 1A, 2A and 3A) or increasing to 2.5 children
per woman of childbearing age during the decade 1975-1985

(scenarios 1Z, 1, 2, and 3). For those scenarios with a replacement level fertility rate the fertility rate was assumed
to change smoothly from the present rate to 2.1 children per
woman of childbearing age by 1985 and remain at that level.
For the other scenarios the fertility rate was assumed to
increase smoothly to 2.5 by 1985, remain at that level until
2000, and then gradually return to replacement level by 2025.

Age specific fertility rates were assumed to be directly
related to the total fertility rate and this relationship was
assumed to change gradually with time. For all scenarios it
was assumed that with time childbearing would be distributed
somewhat more evenly across the childbearing years rather
than being as highly concentrated in the 20-30 year age
groups as it is today.

For scenarios 3 and 3A it was assumed that a delay in
the onset of puberty would be associated with the anti-aging
technologies. Therefore, for those scenarios the fertility
rate of women 19 years of age or younger was reduced by 15
percent and fertility at other ages was increased proportion-
ally in compensation. Male births as a percentage of total
births were assumed to remain constant at 51 percent.

Demographic Effects

Because we assumed that life-extending technologies
would have to be administered to prepubescent individuals to
be effective, these technologies did not produce demographic
consequences until well into the next century. The curve
squaring technologies, however, showed some near-term effects.
Table 5 summarizes the projected demographic effects in the
United States and the world. In this table the base case
(scenario 1) is compared with a pure curve squaring case
(scenario 1A). For the United States current trends suggest
that by the year 2025 the number of people over 65 years of
age will have risen from 22 million to 46 million, or from
10 percent to 14 percent of our population. If squaring
technologies come to fruition, as we suspect, by 2025 there
are likely to be 74 million people over 65, comprising 23
percent of our population. By the year 2000, assuming that
the squaring technologies have been introduced, life expectancy at birth will rise to 86 years (versus 72 years in 1975).

Taking a world view, the number of people over 65 years
of age seems likely to grow from 227 million in 1975 to 760
million by 2025, or from 5.8 percent of world population to
9.8 percent. With acceleration of disease curing technologies
represented by our "squared" case, the number of people over
the age of 65 seems likely to grow to about 1.2 billion

Table 5

DEMOGRAPHIC EFFECTS

	(Millions)		
	1975	2000	2025
UNITED STATES			
Base			
Total Population	214	276	329
Over 65	22	33	46
Percent over 65	10%	12%	14%
Squaring			
Over 65	22	38	74
Percent over 65	10	14	23
WORLD			
Base			
Total Population	3900	5800	7700
Over 65	227	425	760
Percent over 65	5.8%	7.3%	9.8%
LDCs	2800	4600	6400
Developed Countries	1100	1200	1300
Squaring			
Over 65	227	475	1200
Percent over 65	5.8%	8.0%	14.4%
LDCs	2800	4700	6800
Developed Countries	1100	1200	1500

people by the year 2025, about 14.4 percent of world
population.

One effect of the disease curing technologies will be
to increase world population. In our demographic model we
found that current trends suggest world population will grow
from about 4 billion at present to 7.7 billion by the year
2025. With the new curve squaring technologies, world population by 2025 will be some 8.3 billion, or 600 million
people more than the base case. Of these 600 million, 400
million will be in less developed countries and 200 million
in developed countries.

To illustrate the consequences of the assumptions in
one of the more "far out" scenarios, Figure 2 is a three
dimensional representation of the population in scenario 2A.
This scenario, it will be recalled, involves both squaring
of the survival curve and life span extension of approximately 15 years. The height of the surface indicates the
number of people, the horizontal axis indicates the age, and
the axis disappearing into the page indicates the year. This
presentation clearly illustrates several interesting aspects
of the demography which results from this scenario. People
born during the small baby boom in the 1990s are just beginning to die, at the age of 110, in 2100. The long period
of constant birth rate plus a squared survival curve produces
a homogenous age distribution of the population through ages
of 90-100 years of age. Death rate is low until advanced
age, when it accelerates considerably above death rates
which are currently experienced.

Socioeconomic Consequences

As indicated previously, it seems likely that the number of people over the age of 65 will increase significantly
from now on. This increase will occur even without the advent of new life-extending technologies because the "baby
boom" children born between 1950 and 1970 will reach the age
of 65 between 2015 and 2035. Before the year 2000, at least,
the new technologies are not likely to make much difference
in the number of elderly, and therefore the social and economic impacts of the new technologies--as a result of their
demographic effects--seem likely to be minimal. Of much
more importance to economic and social conditions is the
assumed average retirement age. We felt this issue was significant for this study since the technologies we investigated would be likely to have the effect of increasing vigor
and diminishing the symptoms of aging, in addition to
affecting survival rates. With vigor at a particular age
changed, clearly retirement rates might also change.

AGE COHORT DISTRIBUTION

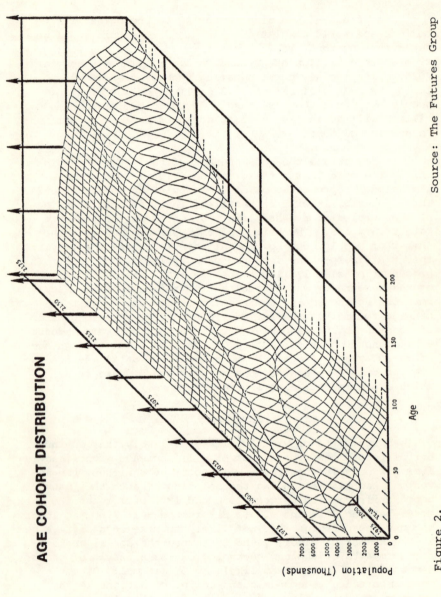

Figure 2.

Source: The Futures Group

We formed the impression that retirement age would be likely to increase for several reasons.

- Polls have indicated that many retired people, when asked, say they would rather be working.

- Feelings of anomie and uselessness which sometime come with retirement apparently accelerate death.

- Both social security and pension funds would benefit appreciably by increasing retirement age only a few years.

- Discrimination on the basis of age, after 65, seemed to us likely to be considered illegal in the near future.

The effect of delayed retirement would include an increase in GNP, diminishing of the dependency ratio, reduced burden on social security, improved socialization among the elderly and--most significantly--a potential problem in the provision of jobs for all those who wished to work. With respect to this latter point, we formed the impression that the nature of work would change: these changes could include the development of more "parallel" jobs, shared work, part-time work, shortening of the work week, and serial careers.

Social Impacts

Examination of social impacts formed a major part of this study. The social impacts considered encompassed a wide range and included, for example, the family, marriage, cohabitation, divorce, consumerism and marketing, education, employment and work, welfare and social assistance, recreation and leisure, crime, politics, urbanization, religion, and communications. We were interested in how the advent of new life-extending technologies might affect such domains of human existence. It was not our purpose to judge whether the consequences foreseen should be encouraged; rather, we sought to identify such impacts, taking into account the many and varied possibilities, and to inquire of people who might feel the effects of these changes as to whether they perceived them to be desirable or not. We used two approaches to identify the impacts. First, we conducted a symposium with insurance company executives at which we inquired about the possible impacts of new life-extending technologies on the insurance industry. We concentrated on the insurance industry because we believe that, of all private institutions, changes in the survival curve would be felt most intimately by the insurance industry. Furthermore, the insurance industry is sensitive to social change, and its products both reflect and seek to anticipate the milieu in which they are set. Second, we conducted interviews with sociologists and social gerontologists. These interviews were preceded by the construction of a taxonomy which covered essentially the entire gamut of social or institutional impacts. In all, this taxonomy included roughly 500 specific effects.

Having identified a subset of impacts of apparent importance, the study team proceeded to inquire about the desirability of these impacts and the actions that might be taken by interest groups in response to them. This portion of the inquiry involved interviews with representatives of interest groups who were asked to provide judgments about impact desirability, possible coalitions with other interest groups, and actions which they might take in response to the evolving impacts.

A number of social impacts may be attributed to the increasing number of older people who will be present even without new technology. Among such effects are the following:

- The aged will have more and more potential political clout as their number and proportion in the population grow, but whether they will translate this potential political power into actual practical influence is doubtful, since the aged will probably remain divided along traditional political lines; even with respect to issues that bear directly on their welfare there probably will be a variety of points of view.

- The nuclear family will continue to decline in importance. On the one hand, family functions will be performed increasingly by extra-familial social mechanisms, such as the school, the church, or the scout troop. In addition, there will be new social forms, particularly to provide family functions to the elderly, such as surrogate families for the "orphaned" elderly. However, life extension will favor reinvigoration of the older tradition of the extended, multigeneration family, since it will reduce the gap in level of vitality between older and younger members of the family.

- Intergenerational marriages will increase. Furthermore, as life extension gives rise to more and more four-generation families, the gap in outlook between

the youngest and oldest generations may prove too
large to bridge comfortably. The second and third
generations may find themselves under particular
pressure, caught between obligations and loyalties
to the oldsters and youngsters.

- New communications technologies will favor reaching
  and influencing those who are homebound or bedridden.
  Education, retraining, entertainment, and information
  about programs and services will all be available
  increasingly through mass communication media such
  as wired-city cable television.

Of course, increasing the number of elderly through the use
of life-extending technologies will have the consequence of
intensifying these impacts.

At present, annual per capita health care costs increase
rapidly with increasing age; therefore, curve squaring will
increase the total cost of health care simply by increasing
the size of the elderly population. However, because curve
squaring probably will increase the health and vigor of all
but the extremely aged, it will tend to reduce per capita
health costs if the costs of the curve squaring technologies
themselves are not considered. Whether, overall, curve
squaring will reduce per capita health care costs thus depends on whether curve squaring is achieved mainly by prevention (which will be relatively inexpensive) or by new,
high technology interventions (which will be relatively
expensive).

Recommendations

Some of the principal recommendations made by the study
team are listed below.

- Studies be conducted to help reach an understanding
  of the changing complex interrelationships between
  retirement age and the changing nature of work. We
  believe that changes in retirement age will cause
  fundamental differences in our economy and in the
  way that older people live and view themselves.

- Detailed information be collected and made available
  to other researchers about economic contributions
  and consumption levels made by older people.

- Various agencies of the government include in their
  policy thinking estimates of the consequences of
  their actions on age of retirement. This

recommendation is particularly relevant to policies
followed by the Department of Labor, Social Security
Administration, the armed forces, and state and
local governments. Policies which affect retirement age can have profound and lasting consequences on the nature of our economy. When those
policies tend to diminish retirement age the
inevitable consequence will be increasing dependency ratio and isolation of the aged. There may
be other policies that affect dependency ratios
directly rather than through retirement age; these
should be pin-pointed and understood in terms of
their likely consequences for American society.
These include, for example, policies that delay
entry into the labor force, shortening of the
work week, introduction of sabbaticals and inter-
mittent retirement, and so on.

- Additional study be applied to questions of international impacts of life-extending technologies
and the changing social dimensions that might
accompany these technologies. While such impacts
were suggested in this study, they were beyond the
initial scope determined for this work; nevertheless, they appear to be important, perhaps urgently
so.

- Government estimates of the cost of developing
biomedical technologies should include from the
outset estimates of the cost of producing those
technologies and distributing them in society.
Emphasis in research on span extending technologies
should be given to those which promise to be inexpensive not only for immediate but secondary costs
as well.